LBSCR
Stockbook

by
Peter Cooper

No. 32636 taking water at Newhaven shed, 13th April 1958. Then the oldest BR engine in service, it is now preserved on the Bluebell Railway.
C.R.L. Coles

Front cover: Fenchurch and *Stepney* on the Bluebell Railway.
M. Esau
Back cover: Luggage van No. 2156 (SR) at Horsham 11/8/46 is of the same pattern as the Milk Van preserved at the Bluebell Railway. *D. Cullum*

ISBN 1 870754 13 1

Design and Production by Kingfisher Publications
Typeset by PageMerger, Southampton
Printed by Amadeus Press, Huddersfield, Yorks.

Published by

Runpast Publishing

10 Kingscote Grove, Cheltenham, Glos. GL51 6JX

Contents

Introduction – the LBSCR

The London, Brighton and South Coast Railway (LBSCR, but often referred to as 'the Brighton') was formed in July 1846 by the amalgamation of two earlier companies. The older of these was the London and Croydon Railway, which was authorised in June 1835; it ran from a junction with the London and Greenwich Railway at Corbetts Lane (Rotherhithe), to West Croydon, and opened throughout in June 1839. The later and longer line was the London and Brighton Railway, which was authorised in July 1837 and started from a junction with the London and Croydon line at Norwood; it then ran through East Croydon and Redhill to Brighton, opening throughout in September 1841. Thus the merged railway's initial main line was from London Bridge to Brighton; the alternative London terminus at Victoria came into use in 1860.

The railway expanded to reach its physical limits quite early on, going eastwards to reach Hastings in 1846 and westwards to reach Portsmouth in 1847; this gave it the form of an inverted 'T'. Further expansion took it to other south coast resorts such as Eastbourne, Bognor and Littlehampton, and then built the inverted 'T' out into a triangle with London at its apex and the base extending from Portsmouth to Hastings.

The LBSCR was predominantly a passenger line, with an intensively operated suburban network and a great deal of holiday traffic to the south coast resorts; goods traffic formed only a small part of its overall activity. Starting from 1909 a system of overhead electrification was introduced in the London area, but the subsequent Southern Railway electrification was of the third rail pattern and the LBSCR's electrification was not, in the long run, perpetuated.

When the LBSCR became one of the three major constituents of the Southern Railway in 1923, its influence on the policies of the new railway in matters of locomotives and other rolling stock was slight. The spirit of the old LBSCR mostly endured in less tangible ways.

The LBSCR preserved

The LBSCR attracted more loyalty and affection than most railways, during its lifetime and afterwards, and this gave it an advantage where preservation schemes were concerned; LBSCR items were more likely than most to be preserved. Two pioneering achievements in railway preservation concern the 'Brighton'; in 1927 the locomotive *Gladstone* was the first in Britain to be preserved privately, and in 1960 the Bluebell Railway, a section of the old LBSCR system, became the first standard gauge preserved passenger railway in the country.

But as this railway was hardly in the forefront of rolling stock development at the Grouping in 1923, and was also greatly affected by main line electrification, much of its stock disappeared relatively early. When the preservation movement was getting into its stride in the early 1960s there was not (at least on the mainland) very much to be had. So a railway most of which still exists as a working electrified system is, in most respects, represented by a rather thin collection of rolling stock; there are few locomotive types preserved, and there are not many carriages.

However, one preservation phenomenon dominates the LBSCR picture and contrasts quite remarkably with its sparseness in other respects. The railway is represented in preservation by thirteen locomotives, and ten of these are of William Stroudley's celebrated 'A' class or 'Terriers'. Of a class of fifty small tank locomotives, built between 1872 and 1880 and principally intended for certain London suburban services, no less than ten were preserved. No other British locomotive type of remotely comparable vintage is preserved in anything like these numbers. How did this come about?

'Terriers' had been popular for a long time; they were quite a celebrated class at the time of the Grouping in 1923, and their reputation matured over the decades following. Their special standing derived partly from their being Stroudley locomotives, but other Stroudley classes lasted almost as long without achieving the same level of popular esteem; the last 'D1' tank went in 1951 with relatively little comment, and the last 'E1' tank in BR service followed a decade later, again without attracting a great deal of attention. Clearly there was something special about the 'Terriers'.

Probably the basis for their popularity was their small size, which gave them the special charm of the miniature. Though small they were 'proper' main line locomotives, able to handle passenger workings and achieve considerable speeds; they were by no means small 'industrials', only capable of shunting and a bit of local goods; they had been notably successful both on London suburban traffic and on a variety of rural workings. Their small size also meant that they could operate on lines with severe weight restrictions and lightly laid track; this took them to a number of interesting railway byways, which added greatly to the variety and interest of the 'Terrier' story.

An LBSCR branch line scene was recreated during the Brighton Works centenary celebrations of October 1952. Special trains on the Kemp Town branch were worked by 'A1X' class No. 32636 and a 2-coach LBSCR push-and-pull unit. The locomotive is now preserved – the coaches unfortunately not. The special is heading back to Brighton on 5th October 1952.　　　　*S.C. Nash*

Such small locomotives, many of them still referred to by their down-to-earth Stroudley names, could easily be regarded as living creatures; the very name 'Terriers' invited it. In their last years two of them were the oldest locomotives on the whole of British Railways, and eventually the 'Terriers' were (by a few months) the last operational LBSCR locomotives. It all combined to give them a standing with very few equals on British Railways. They lasted in service just long enough for the private locomotive preservation movement (then at its fledgling stage) to be able to do justice to their high reputation.

But there are other LBSCR items preserved which must also be given recognition. Preserved LBSCR rolling stock is not very widely dispersed, most of it being at a small number of locations in the south of England. The Bluebell Railway has always held to the traditions of the Brighton line as a major feature of its preservation policy, both in purchase of rolling stock and in environmental aspects. The Kent and East Sussex Railway had 'Terriers' almost from the start, and throughout its history; this tradition is upheld in preservation. On the Isle of Wight there existed a physically separate railway system, which over the years took on many of the features of a working museum of pre-grouping Southern Railway stock, with the LBSCR well represented. It is fortunate that a preserved steam railway society came into being that could ensure that at least a sample of this range of ancient stock would be retained.

This book aims to provide a record of the LBSCR rolling stock that still exists. There are three major

sections, for locomotives, carriages and wagons, and the main emphasis is on items which have been formally preserved; some attention is also given to grounded carriage bodies, and to any other units still in service and which may or may not ultimately be preserved. The preserved locomotives, carriages and wagons are described individually, type by type, with the level of detail varying as the quantity of recorded data varies. The accompanying photographs of locomotives aim to show how their appearance changed over the years; the carriage photographs can only give an outline of the vehicles' history, and the photographs of wagons mostly show them as preserved. Dimensions quoted for locomotives are taken from BR engine record cards and other official documents (though official figures for 'Terrier' cylinder diameters are sometimes suspect); carriage dimensions are from LBSCR carriage registers. The number used when referring to any item is that applying at the time in question; where no such time applies, the original LBSCR number is quoted, if it is known.

The fame and popularity of the 'Terriers' has ensured that they have been preserved in good condition; the preserved carriages too, few though they are, have received a good measure of care in preservation; but the preserved wagons, the least glamorous of rolling stock, have in some cases received little attention. Perhaps, by describing what still exists, this book may lead people to concern themselves with the whole spectrum of preserved LBSCR rolling stock.

Preserved LBSCR locomotives

There are thirteen preserved locomotives of LBSCR origin, which is one of the highest figures of any pre-grouping railway. With this many remaining, one would expect that they would present a comprehensive survey of the railway's locomotive practice over the years. But this is not the case. The youngest of the thirteen locomotives dates from 1898, almost a quarter of a century before the Grouping, and all the other twelve were built within the period 1872-82. These twelve are all from the Stroudley era (and most of them from the first half of it); the thirteenth locomotive is a typical example of R.J. Billinton's work, but there is nothing to represent the last two locomotive superintendents, D.E. Marsh and L.B. Billinton. The preserved locomotives rather suggest that the Brighton had no locomotive history after the turn of the century, and this was not so; but it is true to say that none of Stroudley's successors was of comparable stature, and none established a clear alternative approach to locomotive design.

With twelve Stroudley locomotives preserved one might, again, expect a comprehensive survey of his work – but no. There is no 'D1' tank, his most numerous design and arguably his most important, and only one tender locomotive. The ten preserved 'Terriers' mean that the twelve preserved Stroudley locomotives represent only three Stroudley designs. But what they lack in variety of type they certainly make up for in variety of history. Besides the 'natural' owners – LBSCR, Southern Railway and British Railways – seven other companies, including a colliery and a harbour company, owned one or other of these locomotives at some time. The varied lives they led give them part of their special appeal.

With many pre-grouping railways, the locomotives preserved give some indication of the emergence of modern principles of design. But not with the LBSCR, whose survivors reflect the practice of one period only and are mostly of designs which originated in the early 1870s. Stroudley's locomotives were simply the most memorable the railway ever had, and so the most fitting for preservation.

A pioneer indeed! *Stepney*, the first locomotive of the first standard gauge preserved passenger railway in Britain, waits to leave Sheffield Park on a Bluebell Railway special on 3rd August 1983.   *Mike Esau*

William Stroudley (1833-1889)
Locomotive Superintendent 1870-1889

Although William Stroudley did not start his working career in the railway industry, he moved into it at an early age. His first railway job was at the Great Western Railway under Daniel Gooch in 1853, after which he worked on the Great Northern Railway at Peterborough, and was then Works Manager of the Edinburgh and Glasgow (later North British) Railway at Cowlairs. In 1865 he became Locomotive Superintendent of the Highland Railway, and finally in 1870 he took up the appointment of Locomotive Superintendent of the LBSCR at Brighton.

Stroudley invariably designed and built compact locomotives, with inside cylinders; with only one (very late) exception each of them had six wheels. He mostly used the 0-6-0 and 0-4-2 wheel arrangements, and built tender and tank varieties of both. He was particularly noted as an advocate of standardisation, introducing it onto a railway where it had been noticeably absent. Thus he greatly reduced the number of locomotive types, and established a high degree of commonality of parts between these few classes.

Stroudley's locomotives were always well proportioned, with a characteristic copper cap to the chimney. Great attention to detail, rather than any startling innovation in design, was probably the main reason for their success. Except for his goods tender engines, all Stroudley's locomotives were named, and the passenger classes carried his renowned yellow livery, 'improved engine green', otherwise called gamboge or golden ochre.

Stroudley died in office in 1889.

'A' class Nos. 40 *Brighton*, 46 *Newington*, 50 *Whitechapel*, 54 *Waddon*, 55 *Stepney*, 62 *Martello*, 70 *Poplar*, 72 *Fenchurch*, 78 *Knowle* and 82 *Boxhill*

The first locomotives that Stroudley built for the LBSCR, in 1871-72, were a pair of improvised 0-4-2 tanks, followed by four 'Belgravia' 2-4-0s and the first two of his 'C' class goods. These were mostly rather exploratory or interim in nature, and not entirely successful; they were followed by his first undoubted success at Brighton. This was the 'A' class 0-6-0 tank locomotive design, intended for certain London suburban services where lightly laid track imposed serious weight limitations. It was a nicely judged design – light enough to operate over these tracks, but powerful enough to be master of the job. Fifty of the 'A' class, Nos. 35-84, were built between 1872 and 1880.

The first batch of six of the 'A' class were completed in the latter months of 1872, and included two of the survivors of the class. These were No. 72 *Fenchurch*, the first of the class to enter service on 7th September, and No. 70 *Poplar* which entered service on 4th December. They were both based initially at Battersea depot, and both worked for most of their LBSCR careers from there. They were finished in the full finery of Stroudley's golden ochre lined livery, and were put to work on the South London line from Victoria to London Bridge. From their small, wiry appearance and their keenness to attack their work they were very soon acquired the nickname 'Terriers'. Later, when the class was used on the East London line, from New Cross through the Brunel tunnel to Shoreditch, the name was again seen

to be most apt, as it summed up the enthusiasm with which, terrier-like, they dived into the tunnel.

Like most LBSCR locomotives in the early Stroudley years, the 'A' class or 'Terriers' were mostly built in batches of six. Seven batches of 'Terriers' were built between 1872 and 1880, with a few small differences between some batches, and survivors are to be found from five of these batches. The third batch, unusually of twelve locomotives, included No. 62 *Martello*, completed in October 1875, No. 55 *Stepney* in December 1875 and No. 54 *Waddon* in February 1876. All three were allocated to New Cross depot, and all three spent most of the first thirty years of their lives there. The fourth batch (of six) included No. 50 *Whitechapel*, completed in December 1876, and No. 46 *Newington* of January 1877; *Whitechapel* was allocated to New Cross and *Newington* to Battersea and both, again, spent most of the next thirty years at these depots.

The next surviving 'Terrier', from the sixth batch, was a locomotive of some celebrity in the early days. This was No. 40 *Brighton*, completed in March 1878, which carried the name of the town synonymous with the railway, as this was the locomotive sent to the Paris Exhibition of 1878. *Brighton* was awarded a gold medal at the exhibition, and ran for some years with the inscription 'Gold Medal Paris Exhibition 1878' painted on the side tanks above the name. On returning to the more prosaic world of the day-to-day LBSCR, *Brighton*

Early 'Terriers' – the two survivors from the first batch, Nos. 72 *Fenchurch* and 70 *Poplar*, are both seen in Battersea yard. *Poplar*'s photo is labelled '5/7/80', and *Fenchurch*'s also probably dates from about 1880, as both have received Westinghouse brake equipment, but are otherwise largely in original condition.   *R.C. Riley collection*

A prize-winning 'Terrier' – No. 40 *Brighton*, also pictured at Battersea, carries the inscription to record her celebrated visit to France for the Paris Exhibition of 1878. But this photograph was taken several years later, as *Brighton* no longer has the condensing pipes, removed in 1893.   *courtesy National Railway Museum, York*

A later 'Terrier' – No. 78 *Knowle* was one of the final (1880) batch, fitted with metal brake shoes from new. This one also has the condensing pipes removed, and appears to be at Fratton, which dates the photo as probably about 1900.   *Lens of Sutton*

All the previous four retain their original numbers on bunkerside number plates. But when they were renumbered into the 600 series their numbers were applied in other ways. Such a one was No. 655 *Stepney*, with stencilled numerals, seen at Brighton around 1905.   *Lens of Sutton*

Dimensions

Wheel arrangement 0-6-0
Cylinders (2) – bore . . . . (see below)
            stroke . . . . 20"
Driving wheel diameter . . . . 4'0"
Boiler pressure . . . . 150 lb/sq.in
Tractive effort . . . . (see below)
Wheelbase . . . . 12' 0"
Overall length . . . . 26' 0½"
Overall height . . . . 11' 0¼"
Weight in working order . . . . 28 tons 5 cwt
Grate area . . . . 10 sq.ft
Total heating surface . . . . 488.72 sq.ft
Boiler tubes . . . . 119 x 1¾"
Water capacity . . . . 500 gallons
Coal capacity . . . . (various)
Stephenson link motion, slide valves, lever reverse, left hand drive

Service Histories

Type introduced – September 1872
All built by – LBSCR, Brighton
Cost – £1800 each

No. 40

Cylinder bore . . . . 14"   Tractive effort . . . . . 10,412 lbs
Service date . . . .   March 1878 (duplicate list 6/00)
Numbers:-   LBSCR   – 40 (3/78)
              IWCR   – 11 (1/02)
              SR   – W11 (1924), 2640 (6/47)
              BR   – 32640 (3/51)
Withdrawn . . . Sept. 1963   Final mileage 1,164,724

No. 46

Cylinder bore . . . . 14"   Tractive effort . . . . . 10,412 lbs
Service date . . . .   Jan. 1877 (duplicate list 12/99)
Numbers:-   LBSCR   – 46 (1/77), 646 (4/02)
              LSWR   – 734 (3/03)
              FYNR   – 2 (2/17)
              SR   – W2 (3/24), W8 (4/32)
              BR   – 32646 (8/49)
Withdrawn . . . Nov. 1963   Final mileage . . . . . . unknown*

No. 50

Cylinder bore . . . . 12"   Tractive effort . . . . . . 7,650 lbs
Service date . . . .   Dec. 1876 (duplicate list 12/99)
Numbers:-   LBSCR   – 50 (12/76), 650 (6/01)
              SR   – B650 (1/26), W9 (5/30),
                        515S (4/37)
              BR   – DS515 (2/52), 32650 (11/53)
Withdrawn . . . Nov. 1963   Final mileage 1,271,019

No. 54

Cylinder bore . . . . 14"   Tractive effort . . . . . 10,412 lbs
Service date . . . .   Feb. 1876 (duplicate list 6/99)
Numbers:-   LBSCR   – 54 (2/76), 654 (1/00)
              SECR   – 751 (9/04)
              SR   – 680S (12/32)
               BR   – DS680 (10/50)
Withdrawn . . . Feb. 1963   Final mileage . . . . . . unknown*

No. 55

Cylinder bore . . . . 12"   Tractive effort . . . . . 7,650 lbs
Service date . . . .   Dec. 1875 (duplicate list 6/99)
Numbers:-   LBSCR   – 55 (12/75), 655 (6/01)
              SR   – B655 (1/27), 2655 (4/33)
              BR   – 32655 (12/49)
Withdrawn . . . . May 1960   Final mileage 1, 396, 027

No. 62

Cylinder bore . . . . 12"   Tractive effort . . . . . 7,650 lbs
Service date . . . .   Oct. 1875 (duplicate list 12/98)
Numbers:-   LBSCR   – 62 (10/75), 662 (6/01)
              SR   – B662 (3/25), 2662 (1/34)
              BR   – 32662 (9/49)
Withdrawn . . . . Nov. 1963   Final mileage 1,505,955

No. 70

Cylinder bore . . . . 13"   Tractive effort . . . . . 8,978 lbs
Service date . . . .   Dec. 1872 (duplicate list 6/97)
Numbers:-   LBSCR   – 70 (12/72)
              KESR   – 3 (4/01)
              BR   – 32670 (10/49)
Withdrawn . . . Nov. 1963   Final mileage . . . . . . unknown*

No. 72

Cylinder bore . . . . 14"   Tractive effort . . . . . 10,412 lbs
Service date . . . .   Sept. 1872 (duplicate list 12/97)
Numbers:-   LBSCR   – 72 (9/72)
              NHC   – (unnumbered – 6/98)
              SR   – B636 (2/27), 2636 (1/36)
              BR   – 32636 (6/50)
Withdrawn . . . . Nov. 1963   Final mileage 1,109,513

No. 78

Cylinder bore . . . . 14"   Tractive effort . . . . . 10,412 lbs
Service date . . . .   July 1880 (duplicate list 6/05)
Numbers:-   LBSCR   – 78 (7/80), 678 (3/07)
              SR   – W4 (5/29), W14 (9/32),
                        2678 (7/37)
              BR   – 32678 (8/48)
Withdrawn . . . . Oct. 1963   Final mileage 1,389,447

No. 82

Cylinder bore . . . . 12"   Tractive effort . . . . . 7,650 lbs
Service date . . . .   Aug. 1880 (duplicate list 12/05)
Numbers:-   LBSCR   – 82 (8/80), 682 (11/11),
                        unnumbered (2/20)
              SR   – 380S (6/32)
Withdrawn . . August 1946   Final mileage . . . . . . unknown*

* No. 46 ran 574,266 miles up to sale by the LBSCR, and 116,094 miles after return to the mainland, up to final BR overhaul in 1962.

* No. 54 had run 792,239 miles up to August 1921, but no later figures are available.

* No. 70 ran 664,108 miles up to sale by the LBSCR, and 233,058 miles from 1934 to final BR overhaul in 1960.

* No. 82 had run 734,512 miles at the Grouping in 1923, but no later figures are available.

'Terriers' sold – two of the first to be sold were *Fenchurch* and *Poplar*. *Above left: Poplar* became Kent & East Sussex Railway No. 3 *Bodiam* and has acquired some rather primitive coal rails, but is otherwise in 'as sold' condition, with the Westinghouse pump removed. On the other hand *Fenchurch* (*above right*) continued to enjoy the full amenity of overhaul at Brighton Works after sale to the Newhaven Harbour Company. This loco was a fairly early conversion to 'AIX' and is seen in this form, probably about 1920, at Newhaven. *Lens of Sutton*

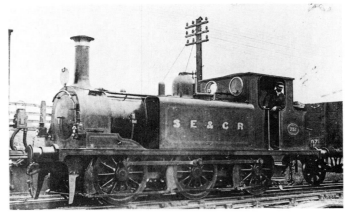

The LBSCR sold four 'Terriers' to the Isle of Wight Central Railway; the third was the celebrated No. 40, which became IWCR No. 11, but remains essentially as sold.
Courtesy of National Railway Museum, York

A 'Terrier' sold to a major company was No. 654 which became South Eastern & Chatham Railway No. 751, and received the full lined-out Wainwright SECR livery. *Lens of Sutton*

The other major constituent of the Southern Railway also bought 'Terriers'. No. 646 became LSWR No. 734 and received Drummond's style of lined livery. The locomotive is in Nine Elms yard, shortly after delivery and repainting, in 1903. *Collection of the late George Kerley*

was sent to work from Battersea depot, and remained there for most, if not all, her LBSCR career.

The other two survivors are from the final batch of eight 'Terriers' built in 1880. These were No. 78 *Knowle*, completed in July, and No. 82 *Boxhill*, completed in August. *Knowle* worked initially from New Cross, but in 1884 left London and was transferred to Tunbridge Wells, moving to Brighton in the early 1890s and to Portsmouth around 1900. *Boxhill* remained a London engine rather longer, being recorded based at New Cross, Croydon and Battersea in the first decade of her life, but then spent most of the 1890s based at Brighton.

The differences between batches of 'Terriers' included the connecting pipes between the tanks, over the firebox, in the first batch; these were removed fairly early. The sixth and seventh batches were fitted with Westinghouse pumps, which later became standard on the whole class, and the seventh batch were built with metal brake shoes, rather than the previous wood, and this again later became standard.

By the mid 1890s the 'Terriers' were still giving good service, mostly in the London area, but times had moved on; they had been fairly small locomotives even by the standards of the 1870s, and were much the smallest of Stroudley's designs. The lightly laid suburban track that had originally called them into being had been replaced, so heavier engines could do the work, and plenty of bigger locomotives were about. Stroudley's own 'D' class tanks, and several of R.J. Billinton's tank locomotive classes, were available and had by this time taken over many of the original 'Terrier' duties. The 'Terriers' now found themselves on lesser duties, and piloting; the need for retaining the whole class of fifty was now questionable.

The first ominous event for the 'Terriers' was in the late 1890s, when they began to be placed on the duplicate list. This was a form of withdrawal from service, though the locomotives remained available for duties. The first 'Terrier' to be put on the duplicate list was No. 70 *Poplar* in June 1897, and No. 72 *Fenchurch* was one of the next, in December 1897. All the 'Terriers' except No. 84 were put on the duplicate list, with No. 82 *Boxhill* being one of the last two, in December 1905. Being on the duplicate list meant that a locomotive's number could be reused for new construction; when the number was actually needed for reuse, the duplicated engine was renumbered into the 600 series, which for all these 'Terriers' simply meant adding 600 to the existing number. One of the first three 'Terriers' to be renumbered was No. 54 *Waddon*, in January 1900, to make way for one of the first Billinton 'B4s'; many of the other 'Terriers' followed suit, and *Boxhill* was the last but one, becoming No. 682 in December 1911.

But not all 'Terriers' followed these apparently inevitable steps, to the duplicate list and then to the 600 series and continuing work on the LBSCR. Between 1898 and 1905 fifteen of them were sold out of service, and another eleven were withdrawn and scrapped. It

was these sales, and others later, which added greatly to the complexity and interest of the 'Terrier' story; five of the ten survivors were among those sold.

The first 'Terrier' to leave LBSCR service was No. 72 *Fenchurch* which was sold in June 1898 for £350 to the Newhaven Harbour Company. The railway system of Newhaven Harbour was not owned by the LBSCR, though the railway company had a controlling interest; the Newhaven company's own small locomotives had not proved entirely satisfactory in service, so it was natural that the LBSCR should provide a replacement. Several 'Terriers' worked at Newhaven in temporary roles before *Fenchurch* arrived on a permanent basis. The job was not very demanding - trains of wagons had to be worked to and from the sidings of the West Quay, and there was some shunting to be done there. In Southern and BR times no other type of locomotive was permitted to work on these lines. *Fenchurch* established herself as part of the Newhaven landscape, being resident from 1898 until 1955 and undergoing several external changes during this period; the engine was given the lined black livery of the Newhaven Harbour Company in about 1910, and later lost the name, which was replaced by the harbour company's title on the tanksides.

No. 70 *Poplar* was recorded sold in April 1901 for £650 'to Mr Stephens, Rother Valley Railway'; he was not yet Colonel Stephens, and the railway was not yet the Kent and East Sussex Railway. The Rother Valley Railway opened in March 1900 from the SECR at Robertsbridge to Tenterden (the present Rolvenden station), and was extended in May 1905 to the SECR at Headcorn. It changed its name in 1904 to the Kent and East Sussex Railway, and aimed to pay its way with passenger traffic and agricultural and general merchandise; there was certainly no mineral or industrial traffic. *Poplar* became the K&ESR's No. 3 *Bodiam* and remained in use until the 1920s, but by about 1930 was in a very dilapidated condition. She was restored to working order in 1932-33 by cannibalising the K&ESR's other 'Terrier' (former No. 671 *Wapping*). No. 3 returned to service in December 1934, no longer carrying a name, and served through the 1930s and 1940s.

A major working location for 'Terriers' was to be the Isle of Wight, and No. 75 *Blackwall* in 1899 was the first 'Terrier' to be sent there. In January 1902 No. 40 *Brighton* became the third of the four 'Terriers' to be sold to the Isle of Wight Central Railway, in this case for £600, becoming the railway's No. 11. The Isle of Wight Central Railway was formed in 1887 by the amalgamation of the Cowes and Newport Railway (the first railway on the Island, opened in 1862), the Ryde and Newport Railway and the Isle of Wight (Newport Junction) Railway, the combined railway constituting the biggest route mileage on the Island. No. 11 received a number of modifications over the years, notably two typical hallmarks of the IWCR; the bunker was extended, eliminating the separate tool box, to increase the coal capacity from 12 cwt to 1½ tons, and the Stroudley chimney, when it wore out, was replaced by one manufactured locally by Wheeler & Hurst of Newport.

These three 'Terriers' were all sold while still retaining their original LBSCR numbers (though all three were on the duplicate list), and to comparatively minor railway companies. The other two survivors sold around this time had been renumbered into the 600 series, and were sold to major railways.

No. 646 *Newington* was sold to the LSWR in March 1903 for £500, along with sister engine No. 668 *Clapham*. They were intended for use on the Lyme Regis branch, and became the LSWR's Nos. 734 and 735 respectively. They worked the first official train on this branch in August 1903, and both continued to work on the branch for the next few years, but were then displaced by larger locomotives. No. 734 was then employed on various odd jobs until reboilered at Eastleigh in September 1912 with a boiler of Drummond pattern. In June 1913 she was sent on hire to the Freshwater, Yarmouth and Newport Railway, on the Isle of Wight, and was purchased by the FYNR in March 1914 for £900 as their No. 2, with the payments for the locomotive being spread over three years. The FYNR opened for goods in 1888, and for passenger traffic the following year. Their train services, between Freshwater and Newport, were operated by the Isle of Wight Central Railway until June 1913, after which the FYNR decided to obtain their own motive power, thus leading to the purchase of 'Terrier' No. 2.

Almost the last 'Terrier' to be sold at this time was No. 654 *Waddon*, which was sold to the SECR in September 1904 for £670, becoming their No. 751. The locomotive was bought for use on the Isle of Sheppey Light Railway, where she took up duties early in 1905 and remained until 1909. In January 1910 a new boiler of Wainwright design was fitted, and No. 751 received motor train equipment for use as a standby to the railway's 'P' class, continuing in this role until 1917. The motor train equipment was then removed, and No. 751 took up shunting duties, at first briefly at Richborough and then at Folkestone Harbour.

For the 'Terriers' remaining on the LBSCR, 1905 was clearly a turning point. Up to then they had been named locomotives, painted yellow, employed on a variety of secondary duties including piloting; they were also being regularly sold out of service or withdrawn and scrapped. From 1905 all this changed; their livery became Marsh's lined umber brown, their names were removed, and there were no more sales for over a decade and no other withdrawals for twenty years; new work had been found for the 'Terriers'. Like so many railways at this time, the LBSCR was experimenting with rail motors, both steam and petrol powered, and wanted to compare these with a small locomotive operating with one or two coaches as a push-and-pull unit. Some railways built new locomotives for the purpose, but the LBSCR had the 'Terriers' ready made. *Boxhill* was one

of the two 'Terriers' used for comparative trials in 1905; both were converted to 2-4-0 tanks and had their cylinders lined down to 9 inches; *Boxhill* ran at this period in an experimental lined green livery.

The comparative trials showed the 'Terriers' with trailers to be the most economical units, so during the next few years almost all the LBSCR's remaining 'Terriers' were converted for motor train operation, though they remained as 0-6-0 tanks, with cylinders lined down to 12 inches; *Boxhill* was converted back to this pattern in February 1913. The other survivors on the LBSCR were accordingly converted to motor train working during this period; three in 1907 – No. 678 (ex *Knowle*) in March, No. 650 (ex *Whitechapel*) in May, and No. 655 (ex *Stepney*) in December – and No. 662 (ex *Martello*), one of the last two converted, in May 1909. The motor train workings were scattered throughout the LBSCR system, so the 'Terriers', mostly London based in their early years, now appeared all over the place; West Croydon, Brighton, Portsmouth (Fratton), Bognor, Littlehampton, Horsham and Tunbridge Wells all had work for motor fitted 'Terriers', and one or other of the survivors spent spells at all these sheds. Around 1912 Nos. 655 and 662 were among a small group of 'Terriers' based at West Croydon for motor train workings in the London area, even including a working into Victoria; No. 662 soon moved on, briefly to Horsham, then to Littlehampton and on to Tunbridge Wells; No. 655 moved to Fratton in the late 1910s. No. 650 mostly alternated between Bognor and Portsmouth (Fratton) during the 1910s, while No. 678 was mostly based at Horsham or Littlehampton during her motor fitted days. This work kept the 'Terriers' busier than they had previously been; in the 1890s a typical 'Terrier' annual mileage was 20-25,000 miles, but in the motor train period it was often about 35,000 miles.

Unlike some of the locomotives purpose-built by other railways for motor train workings, the 'Terriers' were an undoubted success at the work. It gave them a new lease of life, and some of their recorded work was quite sparkling, including several records of speeds of 60 mph and over. This led to the next new development; it was rather unusual for a new type of boiler to be designed for a class on the duplicate list, and then fitted to a large proportion of the surviving locomotives, but this happened to the 'Terriers'. The new pattern of boiler, designed by Marsh, was recognisable by the dome being set further forward than before; fitting of one of these boilers was accompanied by a new extended smokebox on a saddle, and the locomotives treated in this way were reclassified 'A1X', with the unconverted 'A' class becoming the 'A1' class. No. 678 in November 1911 was one of the first two converted, with No. 655 following in October 1912 and No. 662 in December 1913; conversions to 'A1X' continued up to the Grouping, and No. 650 in May 1920 was one of the last converted by the LBSCR. No. 678 retained a copper capped chimney on conversion to 'A1X', but Nos. 655,

The motor train era – the first 'Terrier' to be converted, in 1905, was No. 82 *Boxhill*, seen here in Brighton shed yard as a 2-4-0 tank. The livery is presumably the experimental green – note the different treatment of the corners from the original pattern as in *Brighton*.

F. Burtt collection, National Railway Museum, York

Motor train at work – No. 662 and a 'Balloon' coach are working a Coulsdon-Crystal Palace rail motor near Purley on 7th September 1912. Condensing pipes have been refitted, and coal rails added.

LCGB, Ken Nunn collection

Their work continued as before in the early days of the 'A1X' era. No. 678, one of the first 'A1X' conversions, retained the copper-capped Stroudley chimney with the new extended smokebox, and also has coal rails and condensing pipes.

Lens of Sutton

'Terriers' in Southern green – one of the few to run as an 'A1' in SR livery was No. W2 *Freshwater*, formerly of the Freshwater, Yarmouth and Newport Railway, and before that LSWR No. 734. By 19th August 1931, the date of this photo, the loco was running with a Drummond boiler and an extended bunker, but still retained the Stroudley chimney; this is a Freshwater train (of Stroudley 4-wheelers) at Newport.

S. W. Baker

662 and 650 all acquired the Marsh pattern of cast iron chimney when they became 'A1Xs', No. 655 being the first 'A1X' to receive such a chimney.

Reboilering and conversion to 'A1X' was not limited to the LBSCR's own 'Terriers'; three of those previously sold also received the treatment, with the boilers supplied by Brighton works, and these included the Newhaven Harbour Company's *Fenchurch* in April 1913 and the Isle of Wight Central Railway's No. 11 in May 1918. On the LBSCR, however, No. 682 (ex *Boxhill*) was not converted to 'A1X' but was removed from the duplicate list in February 1920 on taking up duties as an unnumbered pilot at Brighton works.

When the Southern Railway was formed at the Grouping in 1923, the position of the 'Terriers' was quite remarkable. In addition to the sixteen (fourteen 'A1Xs' and two 'A1s'), that the Southern inherited from the LBSCR, the new railway received seven others (two 'A1Xs' and five 'A1s') from four other sources, which included both the other major constituent companies, the LSWR and the SECR. The sixteen from the LBSCR included five of the present survivors (four 'A1Xs' and one 'A1', *Boxhill*) and the other seven included three more survivors. These three were No. 751 from the SECR, No. 11 from the IWCR, and No. 2 from the FYNR. At this point the K&ESR's No. 3 and the Newhaven Harbour Co's *Fenchurch* remained the property of their separate companies, though the

Southern Railway absorbed the Newhaven Company in 1926 and so *Fenchurch* then became a Southern engine.

Among the ex-LBSCR 'A1Xs', Nos. 650 and 655 were based at Fratton at the time of the Grouping, No. 662 was at Tunbridge Wells and No. 678 at Horsham; No. 662 moved in 1925 to start her long stay at Fratton. The normal course of events for a 'Terrier' coming from LBSCR to Southern ownership would be to receive a 'B' (for Brighton) prefix to the number, and lined green Southern livery; Nos. 650 and 662 did so, in January 1926 and March 1925 respectively. But 1925 brought another crisis for the 'Terriers'; a great many Stroudley 'D1' tanks had been converted for motor train working in the early 1920s, and being able to handle heavier loads, some of them displaced 'Terriers' from these duties. Several 'Terriers' were withdrawn; three were cut up, one was sold, and three others, Nos. 655, 677 and 678, were recorded as withdrawn but were in fact placed in store – they were poised on the brink of cutting up, but survived, to be reconditioned and returned to service. No. 655 was the first to be given a reprieve and re-entered service in January 1927 as No. B655 in SR lined green, taking up duties again at Fratton. In March 1927 No. B655 was fitted with LSWR pattern push-and-pull equipment, to operate on the Lee-on-the-Solent branch, but lost this equipment in 1937. In February 1927 *Fenchurch*, reacquired as part of the Southern's purchase of the Newhaven Harbour Co,

The typical Southern 'Terrier' was more like this. 'A1X' class No. B650 is seen during her brief mainland spell (1926-30) before being sent to the Isle of Wight as No. W9. Marsh chimneys were carried by most mainland 'A1Xs' by now, the condensing pipes are still in place, coal rails are fitted, and the wooden brake shoes have been replaced by metal.

M. D. England, courtesy R. C. Riley

Rural railway, Isle of Wight style. No. W11 *Newport* is in action with a train of 4-wheelers, in 1930 or soon after. This is all typical Island 'A1X' stuff of that period – the Wheeler & Hurst chimney, extended bunker, and front splasher sandboxes (indicating a non-Brighton 'A1X' conversion). *M.D. England collection, National Railway Museum, York*

received a 'B' prefix number, but was given lined black goods livery and the number B636, instead of B672 which would have been logical; however, she continued to do the same work as before at Newhaven.

The former *Boxhill*, unnumbered at the Grouping, continued as Brighton Loco Department pilot, and remained in this duty for almost the whole of the Southern era. In 1928 the lined umber livery and copper capped chimney were replaced by plain black and a Marsh chimney, and in 1932 the engine was officially numbered 380S in the departmental list. The other surviving 'A1', the former SECR No. 751, at Folkestone Harbour at the Grouping, went to shunt at Ashford Works briefly in 1924, and was then Battersea loco depot pilot. After this she was stored, in a rather run down condition, from 1926 to 1930 at Preston Park, before being sent, still in SECR wartime livery and still with the SECR replacement boiler, to Eastbourne to supply steam for a pulverised coal plant. This menial task must certainly have seemed like the end of the road, but no – in December 1932 she emerged from a general overhaul at Brighton. She still carried the SECR boiler, but now had an LSWR Drummond chimney and was sent, painted plain black as departmental No. 680S, to be pilot at Lancing Carriage Works. Later, in February 1937, the SECR boiler was replaced by an 'A1X' boiler, but as No. 680S did not receive an extended smokebox she became neither fish nor fowl, not really an 'A1' or an 'A1X'. She continued in the same work at Lancing to the end of the Southern era, and indeed until withdrawal fifteen years after that.

The Isle of Wight was a major stamping ground for 'Terriers' in the Southern era; five were on the Island at the time of the Grouping, and three others were sent there over the next few years. Renumbering of the locomotives inherited from the three Island railways was very simple – the FYNR had only two, Nos. 1 and 2; the IWCR had nine, Nos. 4 to 12; and the IWR's carried names only. So FYNR and IWCR locomotives simply acquired a 'W' prefix to their existing numbers; FYNR 'A1' class No. 2 became SR No. W2 in lined green livery in March 1924, and was fitted with an extended bunker at the same time; IWCR 'A1X' class No. 11 became SR No. W11 also in 1924. Both at this time had non-standard features, No. W2 the LSWR Drummond boiler and No. W11 the locally manufactured chimney.

The 1920s were the period of the main importing of 'O2' class tank engines onto the Isle of Wight, as most of the assorted motive power of the old Island railways was replaced and withdrawn. But there were certain lines on the Island which could not take 'O2s', and for these 'Terriers' were adopted as the standard engine, with three more being sent out to replace some of the older, smaller locomotives. The second of these three was No. 678, taken out of store in 1929, fitted with an extended bunker, Marsh chimney and 14" cylinders and sent to the Island as No. W4 in May that year; there she was given the name *Bembridge*. In 1930 No. B650 followed, and was the last 'Terrier' to be sent to the Island by the Southern; she was likewise fitted with an extended bunker and went out in May 1930 as No. W9, receiving the name *Fishbourne* on arrival. Around the same time the 'Terriers' already on the Island received names, No. W2 becoming *Freshwater* in October 1928 and No. W11 becoming *Newport* in June 1930.

Departmental 'Terriers' – the former *Boxhill* was in departmental use at Brighton Works from 1920 onwards, and in the early 1920s retained a Stroudley chimney with a lined livery.

R.C. Riley collection

Boxhill later received a Marsh chimney, and later still the Drummond pattern, as seen here on 29th June 1946. This was her final running condition, and two months later she was withdrawn for preservation. Since 1932 she had been numbered 380S in the departmental list, but had been painted unlined black since 1928.

H.C. Casserley

An unlikely workplace for an ex-Isle of Wight 'Terrier' was Lancing Carriage Works, where the former No. W9 *Fishbourne* (previously No. B650) was sent in 1937, remaining there until 1953. Unusually for a departmental locomotive, she was given lined green livery, and looks very smart when photographed on 17th June 1939 at Lancing.

S.W. Baker

The last Southern loco to retain a pre-Grouping livery was the ex-SECR 'Terrier', in wartime utility grey on 21st February 1932. At this time she was serving as a stationary boiler (the 1911 SECR replacement boiler, in fact) at Eastbourne.

S.W. Baker

No. 751 became departmental No. 680S, and later DS680, receiving plain black livery, a Drummond chimney, and (later) an 'A1X' boiler. The loco looks plain but passably smart in BR days.

Lens of Sutton

The early 1930s were the heyday of the 'Terriers' on the Isle of Wight. Seven of them were there from 1930, principally employed on the Freshwater, Ventnor West and Bembridge branches. A few changes occurred around 1932. No. W2 received a new boiler and smoke-box to convert her to 'A1X' in March 1932, and was renumbered W8 and given an LSWR pattern of chimney, as this was being adopted as a standard for Isle of Wight locomotives. No. W11 also received such a chimney about this time, and so did No. W4, which was renumbered W14 in late 1932; but No. W9 retained the Marsh chimney. The allocations of 1933 show No. W9 at Ryde (with No. W13) for the Bembridge branch, and Nos. W8, W11 and W14 among Newport's allocation mainly to cover the Freshwater line and the Ventnor West branch.

This 'Terrier' heyday came to an end in 1936; upgrading of the Freshwater and Bembridge branches meant that 'O2s' could now operate these lines. The main need for 'Terriers' was now on the Ventnor West line, so four of the seven were returned to the mainland, handing over their names to the four 'O2s' that were sent out to replace them. The four 'Terriers' sent back included Nos. W9 and W14, which were dumped in Eastleigh yard; things did not look promising for them, but two of the four survived. No. W9 was the first to find new work, being overhauled at Eastleigh, repainted in lined green, renumbered 515S in the departmental list and sent in April 1937 to join No. 680S as a pilot at Lancing Carriage Works. As No. 678, W14 had been withdrawn in 1925, and reinstated in 1929; she was again withdrawn in December 1936, but was again reinstated; she was given a general overhaul and was sent in June 1937 as No. 2678 to augment the 'Terrier' numbers at Fratton. Only three 'Terriers', Nos. W8, W11 and W13, remained on the Island up to and through the war, by which time No. W8 had received a Marsh chimney.

The high summer of the Southern branch line is pictured in this view of No. 2678 heading away from Havant on a Hayling Island branch train. For a locomotive which had been withdrawn and reinstated twice at this point, she looks very well. She carries a Drummond chimney and extended bunker as relics of her seven year stay on the Isle of Wight, and briefly worked on the Hayling branch in the late 1930s, before her 18 year spell on the K&ESR.
G.H. Soole collection, National Railway Museum, York

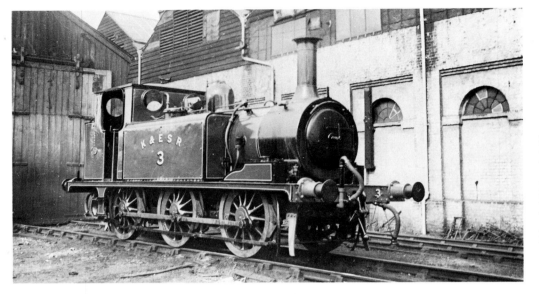

K&ESR 'Terrier' No. 3 re-entered service in 1934, and was converted to 'A1X' in 1944. After overhaul at Brighton Works, she was repainted in K&ESR lined green livery, in this case a slightly darker green than SR malachite, and is about to return to the K&ESR on 13th September 1947. *S.C. Nash*

While the Island 'Terrier' operation waxed and waned, their main base on the mainland had been Fratton, where they principally worked the Hayling Island branch; this, like the Newhaven Harbour system, was a line where they were the only type permitted. The 4½ mile branch from Havant to Hayling Island was opened in 1867, and 'Terriers' had operated it since the early 1890s. Here Nos. B655 and B662 had been residents for several years, becoming Nos. 2655 and 2662 in April 1933 and January 1934 respectively. They were two of the regular allocation of 'Terriers' at Fratton in the 1930s, along with Nos. 2635 and 2661 and later additions, including No. 2678. By the late 1930s the Southern was well enough stocked with 'Terriers' to be able to lend one or two. On the Kent and East Sussex Railway, on the other hand, the motive power situation was now such that it needed to borrow locomotives; 'Terrier' No. 3 was one of a diminishing group of useable locomotives. Three of Fratton's 'Terriers' spent time on the K&ESR – the first was No. 2655, which the

K&ESR hired from August 1938 to October 1939. The third 'Terrier' sent to the K&ESR stayed by far the longest; No. 2678 was hired in February 1940 and remained on the line until nationalisation and for a further ten years after that. Meanwhile at Newhaven No. B636 had become No. 2636 in January 1936, with LBSCR pattern numerals but still in black livery, and shared this duty with No. 2647 for many years.

The latter days of the Southern Railway saw most of the 'Terriers' painted in plain black with 'sunshine' lettering; one exception was No. 2655 which received unlined dark green livery, with lettering in the Bulleid style, in December 1939, and retained this until around the end of the war. A few other events can be recorded along the way. In March 1944 K&ESR No. 3 was converted to 'A1X' and was the very last such conversion – remarkably, this was done in St. Leonards loco shed; she then continued to be a mainstay of the line. Late in 1945 the Brighton Works pilot No. 380S was rather altered in appearance by receiving a Drummond

In the later days of the Southern most of the 'Terriers' were repainted plain black. A good example is No. 2640 (ex W11), newly returned from the Isle of Wight and overhauled at Eastleigh, where she is pictured in the Works on 5th July 1947. *R.C. Riley*

chimney, but in August 1946 this locomotive was withdrawn for preservation. After the war the short-lived railway oil burning project was under way, and an improbable participant was Lancing Works shunter No. 515S, which was converted to burn oil in September 1946. This exercise was unsuccessful, and the locomotive was converted back to coal burning a year later; around the same time she finally lost the prewar Maunsell lined green livery and was repainted plain black. The final year of the Southern saw an addition to the numbers of mainland 'Terriers' when No. W11 *Newport* returned from the Isle of Wight in April 1947; she became No. 2640 and joined the band working at Fratton, taking up duties there in July after overhaul at Eastleigh.

For the 'Terriers', the formation of British Railways was almost a repeat of the 1923 Grouping; again the newly formed organisation inherited 'Terriers' from several sources – three this time, the Southern, the Kent & East Sussex Railway and the Great Western. Fourteen 'Terriers' passed from Southern to BR ownership, and eight of these survive; the ninth survivor was No. 3 from the K&ESR and the tenth was *Boxhill*, already preserved at this point. Now for the first time since the 1890s all the surviving active 'Terriers' were under the same ownership. The next year the last two Island 'Terriers', Nos. W8 and W13, were displaced from the Ventnor West services and returned to the mainland; No. W8, which had regained her previous Stroudley pattern chimney during the war, became BR No. 32646, taking her correct number in the 'Terrier' sequence. All the Southern Region's 'Terriers' were now in the same working environment, and could interchange among the same collection of duties, if required.

In due course they acquired 30000 series numbers and lined black livery. The first among the survivors to be renumbered was No. 2678, which became No. 32678 in August 1948 but remained in SR plain black livery. The first to receive BR lined black were Nos.

32662 and 32678 in September 1949, but BR crests were not available at this point so both ran with blank tank sides. The following month K&ESR No. 3 was renumbered 32670, her correct number in the 'Terrier' sequence, but retained her green livery, again with blank tank sides. No. 32655 was the first to receive the first pattern BR crest in December 1949, and Nos. 32636 and 32640 received full BR lined black and crests on being renumbered in June 1950 and March 1951 respectively. Last among the present survivors to receive proper BR livery were No. 32646, which retained the legend 'BRITISH RAILWAYS' on the tank sides until December 1951, and No. 32670 which finally lost the green livery in March 1954. The two 'Terriers' at Lancing were likewise renumbered into the DS series, remaining in unlined black; No. 680S was renumbered DS680 in October 1950, while No. 515S became DS515 in February 1952. A most unusual development for No. DS515 followed in November 1953, when the locomotive was transferred out of departmental stock into normal running stock, to take the correct number 32650, receiving lined black livery at the same time.

The physical appearance of these engines was distinctly various; it was commented in the 1950s that no two 'Terriers' were exactly alike. The variations largely reflected their varied histories, as could be seen by considering four aspects – if a 'Terrier' had been converted to 'A1X' at Brighton, it would have separate front sandboxes, while if converted elsewhere the front sandboxes would be integral with the front splashers; if the locomotive had served on the LBSCR in the motor train days it would have 12 inch cylinders, otherwise it would have 14 inch cylinders; if it had served on the Isle of Wight it would have an extended bunker, but if not would retain the original small bunker. Chimneys were a bit more complicated; most ex-Isle of Wight 'Terriers' had Drummond chimneys, while most that had remained on the mainland in LBSCR and SR ownership had the Marsh pattern; but some retained the Stroudley

Interim BR liveries – (left) No. 32646 (formerly W8) retained plain black livery with a simple tankside inscription, on return from the Isle of Wight. Seen at Eastleigh on 14th August 1949, soon after return to the mainland. No. 32662 (right) was the first 'Terrier' to receive the lined black livery, but at a time (September 1949) before BR lion-and-wheel crests were available. Seen at Fratton on 29th May 1950. These two show a wide range of differences – of chimney, bunker, and front splashers, and No. 32646 has the front steps only fitted to latterday Island 'Terriers'.

W. Gilburt/K.J. Robertson collection

The full new regalia – the 'Terriers' eventually received the standard BR lined black livery; here No. 32636, Newhaven's oldest resident, pauses during her work on the West Quay on 12th July 1950. This was the only 'Terrier' to retain the original small bunker, without coal rails, to the end. *R.C. Riley*

copper cap. There were a few exceptions to all this – No. 32678's 14" cylinders were 'wrong' for an old motor train loco, and No. 32662, never an Island engine, acquired the extended bunker from withdrawn No. 32677 (ex W13) in March 1961.

Under British Railways there remained three main areas of work for 'Terriers' in normal running stock. Despite their great age, they were the only locomotives light enough and suitable for these duties; encountering them at, say, Havant, it was amazing to realise that locomotives so small were still doing serious work. Their largest operation was the Hayling Island branch, where peak services in the 1950s called for three 'Terriers' at work on certain days. The locomotives for the Hayling branch remained based at Fratton until this depot closed in November 1959, after which they were based at Eastleigh, with one of them often stabled

overnight at Fratton. For the Kent & East Sussex operation two active 'Terriers' were adequate in normal circumstances; the locomotives on the line were based at Rolvenden, which BR classed as a sub-shed of Ashford; after the northern section of the K&ESR closed in 1954 they were based at St. Leonards. The Newhaven operation remained, as it had always been, a job requiring only one active 'Terrier'; Newhaven shed closed in September 1955, and after this the 'Terriers' on the duty were based at Brighton, one of them being stabled at Newhaven and returning at fortnightly intervals for washouts. In the 1950s there were sufficient 'Terriers' to give spare engines for all these duties, and a typical allocation would be five at Fratton, three on the K&ESR and two at Newhaven, though this varied somewhat.

The first 'Terrier' to receive lined black with a BR crest was No. 32655, which worked on the K&ESR line in the final period of passenger operation there. Here the locomotive brings a mixed train into Robertsbridge on 27th July 1953. *R.C. Riley*

In BR days the biggest 'Terrier' operation was the Hayling Island branch, with intensive services on summer weekends in the final years. No. 32650, a regular on the line for the last ten years of operation, is seen at work on the line on 27th June 1954.   *S.C. Nash*

This is the final condition of the last remaining 'Terriers', in BR lined black livery with the second pattern of crest, but they didn't always look as smart as this. No. 32646 is just ex-works at Brighton on 7th March 1958, having been the last locomotive to receive a general overhaul in the Works there.
                                                                W.M.J. Jackson

Among these duties the surviving 'Terriers' circulated. No. 32636 remained at Newhaven until the shed closed in 1955, but a month later began a four year spell on the K&ESR; she then worked briefly at Hayling Island before a three year stay at Brighton and a few final months at Hayling again. No. 32640 was about the most travelled of the post-war 'Terriers'; she went to the K&ESR in July 1948 and alternated between there and Newhaven until 1954, after which she alternated between the Hayling and Newhaven duties, ending up at Brighton. No. 32646 limited herself to alternating fairly regularly between Fratton (where she went in 1949 on return from the Isle of Wight) and Newhaven, with the last 7½ years spent on the Hayling services. No. 32650 was the simplest case, being a Hayling locomotive throughout after her return to normal running stock. No. 32655 had been a Fratton resident for many years, but moved to the K&ESR services in 1953 and on to Brighton late in 1955, with a final token stay at Eastleigh before withdrawal in 1960. No. 32662, likewise a long time Fratton resident, moved to the Newhaven duties in 1955 for almost eight years before finally returning to the Hayling services. No. 32670's attachment to the K&ESR continued to the start of 1958, and she then spent five years at Brighton before finishing at Hayling. No. 32678 remained on the K&ESR duties until the closure of St. Leonards depot in 1958, then going to the Hayling branch and ending up briefly at Brighton.

The K&ESR services were the first casualties among these 'Terrier' duties. Passenger services ended on the line on 2nd January 1954, with Nos. 32655 and 32678 active on the last day. The surviving freight services operated from St. Leonards until that depot closed in June 1958, with Nos. 32636 and 32678 in the final allocation; at the same time a diesel took over the remaining K&ESR goods duties. No. 32636 went for a while to Ashford as standby for this diesel, but left in August 1959, having been the last 'Terrier' allocated to K&ESR work. With no K&ESR commitments, some 'Terriers' were now surplus to requirements, and one was included in the 1960 condemnation programme. Thus No. 32655 came to be withdrawn and sold to the Bluebell Railway in May 1960.

The Hayling and Newhaven duties continued, with 'Terriers' also helping out at Lancing and occasionally appearing on special workings on the K&ESR. But in 1963 the end finally came; nevertheless, No. 32650 was given a general overhaul in March 1963, the last 'Terrier' to receive such treatment from BR. In April 1963 the first 'USA' tank arrived to take over at Lancing, but No. DS680 had left Lancing on 23rd February, and No. 32662 had stood in during the interim. In August the Newhaven West Quay lines closed; No. 32678 operated the last trip and on 5th October 1963 was the last 'Terrier' to leave Brighton. No. 32640 was withdrawn in September 1963 and No. 32678, for the third and final time, in October; this left only the five at Eastleigh on the Hayling Island duties.

Closure of the Hayling Island branch had been threatened for some time, and the last day of normal operation was Saturday 2nd November 1963, with Nos. 32650/62/70 in action; the specials on the branch the next day were handled by Nos. 32636 and 32670. After that final weekend the five survivors, Nos. 32636/46/50/62/70, were withdrawn, and the 'A1X' class was finally gone from British Railways stock. The oldest of them, No. 32636, was 91 years old.

A classic locomotive type, a legend in its own working lifetime, had passed from the British Railways scene. Already three of the type had been preserved, ensuring that 'Terriers' would not be gone completely, and it seemed probable that more would be saved, now that their service days were at an end.

The last day – the two oldest locomotives on British Railways, 'A1X' class Nos. 32636 and 32670, at Fratton Motive Power Depot on 3rd November 1963. They are about to leave with their train for Havant, to operate the very last workings over the Hayling Island branch. By this time both locomotives had received 'diesel' type numerals on their bunker sides. *Bluebell RPS Archives*

The First 'Terrier' Preservations

The enduring popularity of the 'Terriers' meant that they were certain to be one of the first locomotive types to be considered for preservation. What could not be predicted was that they would be preserved in such large numbers. Preserving a lot of 'Terriers' does not really recreate the typical latter day Southern branch line scene, but rather, perhaps, a romanticised version of it. For their last thirty or forty years of service on the Southern Railway and on British Railways they had been limited to a very few specialist jobs, though the Kent and East Sussex Railway and the Isle of Wight railway system do happen to have been two of their specialist locations. What the preservation of so many 'Terriers' does reflect is the great esteem and regard that was felt for them; though ten are preserved, there are still people to be heard lamenting that this or that other 'Terrier' (old *Morden* perhaps, or *Portishead*) was not preserved as well.

The first recorded attempt at 'Terrier' preservation seems to have been in 1939, when it was reported that ex-Shropshire & Montgomeryshire Railway No. 9 *Daphne* (No. 83 *Earlswood*) which the Southern Railway had bought apparently for spares, might instead be restored as a static exhibit at Brighton station. The war then intervened, and the idea evaporated. But very soon after the war a new idea was put forward. At a meeting of the SR Locomotive, Carriage & Wagon and Electrical Committee on 24th July 1946 it was reported that as there were now only fifteen 'Terriers' left 'and in view of the public interest that has always been attached to them' one should be preserved. The former *Boxhill*,

No. 380S, being the only true 'A1' class still on the Southern's books, was earmarked. It was proposed that the locomotive be restored externally as near as possible to original condition. The cost of restoration was estimated at £250 (the scrap value was quoted as £125) and subject to appropriate approvals it was agreed to proceed.

No. 380S was withdrawn from departmental stock on 31st August 1946, and was taken into Brighton Works for restoration work to commence. The changes made included the replacement of the Drummond chimney by one of the Stroudley pattern, refitting of condensing pipes, and modifications to lamp irons and hand rails. When the mechanical work had been done, the locomotive was sent, late in November, to Lancing for painting in Stroudley livery. She remained at Lancing while livery details and other points were sorted out, and returned to Brighton in time to participate in the Works' 1000th locomotive celebrations on 9th June 1947.

Now fully restored as No. 82 *Boxhill*, she left Brighton on 3rd September 1947 under her own steam, to take part in an exhibition at Dorking; she then proceeded to Nine Elms, where she was stored under tarpaulins. The following February *Boxhill* ventured out again to Horsham for the centenary celebrations of the line from there to Three Bridges, and then in June appeared at the centenary celebrations at Waterloo station. The relevance of a preserved LBSCR locomotive at this event could be questioned, but *Boxhill* was always a welcome sight on such occasions.

The first 'Terrier' to be preserved was the former Brighton Works shunter *Boxhill*, which was restored in 1946-47. In the years following she often appeared at Works Open Days and similar events, before being refurbished and going to the National Railway Museum at York. This is at an Open Day at Eastleigh, 17th September 1959, and by this time the original restoration is looking a bit worn. *J.H. Aston*

The Waterloo celebrations marked the beginning of a long lived partnership, for it was here that *Boxhill* first appeared with the ex-LSWR preserved 'T3' class 4-4-0 No. 563, and both locomotives were then stored at Farnham carriage sheds. They became inseparable for many years, except when *Boxhill* went to Brighton Works for further attention in the early months of 1949. During all these travels *Boxhill* had proceeded under her own steam, but after lengthy storage at Farnham her condition deteriorated and she was henceforth a static exhibit. *Boxhill* and the 'T3' now became museum pieces, appearing at such events as Eastleigh Works open days (in 1954, 1955 and 1957), until some more permanent display location could be found.

In April 1958 *Boxhill* and the 'T3' were despatched to Tweedsmouth for storage, but they returned in August 1959, as the prospect of the Museum of British Transport, at Clapham, was now in the air. By summer 1960 it became known that *Boxhill* was to go to the Clapham museum, and in August she entered Eastleigh works for overhaul in readiness for this. At the end of January 1961 *Boxhill* left Eastleigh for Clapham, and remained an exhibit there until the museum closed. In April 1975 *Boxhill*, with the 'T3' as always, was taken to York, and was placed on display in the main hall, where she has been on view most of the time since. As the senior preserved 'Terrier', *Boxhill* represents a point of reference with which all the others can be compared.

The second 'Terrier' to be preserved reflects quite a different aspect of railway preservation. The group which was to become the Bluebell Railway Preservation Society first met in March 1959; they were mainly LBSCR enthusiasts, who aimed to preserve a rural 'Brighton' branch line. For motive power an LBSCR locomotive would clearly be preferred, and in view of their great popularity a 'Terrier' was the obvious first choice. When negotiations had proceeded far enough to think about actually purchasing a locomotive, the Society approached British Railways who said they could have 'Terrier' No. 32655 for £550.

The locomotive arrived at the Bluebell Railway on 17th May 1960. She had been repainted plain black, with no mark of ownership, and with the original number 55 painted on the bunker sides. A copper capped chimney (understood to be from No. 32670) had been fitted. This arrival, with the newly formed railway's first two coaches, was an historic moment in British steam railway preservation. Locomotive and coaches were soon in regular service, following re-opening of the line on 7th August, and the locomotive's name *Stepney* was painted on the tank sides. During the following winter the plain black livery was replaced by the Stroudley golden ochre passenger livery which this locomotive has carried ever since, though it is not really authentic on an 'A1X'.

Through the seasons 1961-67 *Stepney* remained in regular use on the Bluebell Railway, the most obviously Stroudley locomotive on the line. By the end of the 1967 season, this constant use meant the locomotive needed a major overhaul, and she was set aside until this could happen; nobody realised then that it would be fifteen years before *Stepney* was in action again, the whole of the 1970s passing with the locomotive out of service. In the late 1970s the 'face' of another well known tank engine was painted on the smokebox door of the out-of-use *Stepney*; this became the focus around which fund raising built up and enabled the locomotive to be overhauled and returned to service in September 1982.

In the seasons following, *Stepney* has continued to be the only active locomotive in Stroudley livery; she has remained in regular use, though the Bluebell Railway's services in the 1980s and 1990s mostly call for more substantial motive power.

The third 'Terrier' to be preserved introduced a new element to the story – an international element. No. DS680 continued to work at Lancing Carriage Works until late May 1962, and then proceeded to Brighton, where she was presented to the Canadian Railway Historical Association (CRHA) on 4th June. The CRHA is the oldest and largest railway historical society in Canada, and one of its projects is the Canadian Railway Museum at St. Constant, on the outskirts of Montreal.

The locomotive did not go immediately to Canada but instead returned to Lancing shortly after the presentation. She was back at Brighton again on 27th December 1962 and, as a first step towards more authentic LBSCR appearance, the Drummond chimney was replaced by the copper capped chimney (actually a Marsh chimney with copper cap added) taken from No. 32635 which, as No. 377S, had been *Boxhill's* successor as Brighton Works pilot. With this chimney, No. DS680 was used briefly as Brighton coal pilot but returned to Lancing on 2nd February 1963. Three weeks later she left Lancing for good, and shortly afterwards entered Eastleigh Works for overhaul, to be restored (as near as possible) to original condition.

The restored locomotive, with Stroudley pattern copper capped chimney and in Stroudley livery as No. 54 *Waddon*, was outshopped by Eastleigh Works on 4th August 1963, and was on display at the Eastleigh Works Open Day shortly after. Other modifications included fitting the original pattern of clacks, discontinuous handrails, and condensing pipes, but the Marsh 'A1X' boiler remained inconsistent with the Stroudley livery; *Waddon* was still not really an 'A1' or an 'A1X'.

Later the same month *Waddon* was loaded onto a well wagon and left Eastleigh to be taken aboard ship at London Docks, and sailed for Canada. Since arrival there she has been at the Canadian Railway Museum, either on display or in store. She is the oldest locomotive in the museum, and one of the three European locomotives in their collection, the other two being 'A4' class No. 60010 *Dominion of Canada* and an SNCF 0-6-0. There are no plans to return *Waddon* to working order.

Early days in the steam preservation movement – with the spectators obligingly in 'period' clothes. The Bluebell Railway's *Stepney*, with the preserved 'Chesham' carriage set, on 1st April 1962.

C.R.L. Coles

'Terrier' for export – *Waddon*, restored to something like original condition after years of work as a Lancing Works shunter, is swung on board ship at London Docks. She was then taken to Canada, where she resides in the Canadian Railway Museum, near Montreal.

R.C. Riley collection

Preserving the Others

The position in the early months of 1963 was that three 'Terriers' had been preserved, and ten remained in BR service. But it was known that the remaining 'Terrier' duties were likely to come to an end before very long. Withdrawals began in April, and around then three 'Terriers' were taken out of service and all three were cut up – No. DS681 (former No. 32659) in June and Nos. 32635 and 32661 in September. Suddenly the story changes. With only seven 'Terriers' left in BR service, and their withdrawals starting, the full significance of the situation seems to have dawned on all concerned; all these seven 'Terriers' were preserved.

The last 'Terriers' were withdrawn in November 1963, and on 4th January 1964 No. 32662 brought No. 32636 back from Fratton to Eastleigh, so all the class were now gathered there, awaiting sale and despatch. The going rate for these 'Terriers' appears to have been £750, and there was no shortage of takers. The first three preserved 'Terriers' had all been restored to Stroudley yellow livery; with the later seven a great deal more variety of livery was going to be seen in preservation. The first two 'Terriers' to be despatched from Eastleigh to new owners were, appropriately, the two oldest.

The first was No. 32670, which was bought privately by two supporters of the proposed Kent & East Sussex preserved railway. This was a particularly appropriate locomotive for this line. The 'Terriers' were one of the types most favoured for use on the Colonel Stephens railways, and back in 1901 this very locomotive had been the first 'Terrier' bought by the Colonel. As K&ESR No. 3 she had by far the longest record of service of any 'Terrier' on a Colonel Stephens line, and was still serving there in 1948 when the line was absorbed into British Railways. She is now the only surviving K&ESR locomotive; if this railway and this locomotive are both to be preserved, then they clearly belong together.

After being sold, No. 32670 proceeded from Eastleigh to Brighton on 10th April 1964, and continued on to Robertsbridge, via Hastings, the next day. However, the future of the K&ESR preserved line was uncertain for several years, and it was not until 1974 that the official reopening took place. At first No. 32670 remained in BR lined black, resuming her old K&ESR number 3 simply by having '2670' painted out. She was in action at Easter 1966 on the first 'official' train since the 1961 closure of the line; in 1968 she was repainted as No. 3 in the light green livery adopted by the line, and in 1969 the name *Bodiam* was reinstated.

Following a light overhaul in summer 1972, No. 3 was in steam at her centenary celebrations at Rolvenden on 4th November 1972. She then continued to be available for service most of the time until withdrawn in September 1977 for major repairs; during this period she had participated in fellow 'Terrier' No. 10 *Sutton's* centenary celebrations in September 1976. After completion of boiler repairs the locomotive re-entered service on 8th September 1984 in BR lined black livery as No. 32670, but was withdrawn at the end of 1985 requiring further heavy repairs.

The next 'Terrier' to be sold was (and is) considered rather special. No. 32636 had been the oldest locomotive on the Southern Railway and Southern Region for the last thirty years of service, and the oldest on the whole of British Railways during the last few years. If we set aside one or two operable locomotives which have spent long periods as static exhibits, No. 32636, *Fenchurch* of 1872, remains the oldest operational standard gauge locomotive in Britain with a record of continuous service.

In the first few years of its life the Bluebell Railway Preservation Society was very conscious of the need to preserve selected items from the considerable range of historic locomotives which were disappearing from the scene in the early 1960s. Lists were prepared of items which should be pursued, and it is not surprising that by mid 1962 No. 32636 had appeared on such a list; perhaps it only took so long because the railway already had a 'Terrier', and obtaining another did not immediately spring to everyone's mind as the first priority, if a cross-section of historic items was being sought.

The Bluebell RPS fixed their sights on No. 32636, and in early 1964 they purchased the locomotive for the standard fee of £750. At 24 hours notice on 13th May 1964 No. 32636, with the LBSCR milk van the railway had also purchased, arrived via the Ardingly link line, and made up the very last train to use this line. The track over much of this line was lifted shortly after.

Being an operational locomotive, No. 32636 could go into immediate service on the Bluebell line – and did so; indeed, in those days this was normally a requirement of any locomotive accepted onto the line. Surface appearances changed quite rapidly; the '3' at the start of the number was very soon painted out (exactly the opposite of what happened to No. 32670), and so were the BR insignia. The locomotive was renamed *Fenchurch* at a ceremony on 12th July 1964, and by this time had acquired a new livery which, with some modification, was to remain for over twenty years. This was essentially the Newhaven Harbour Company's livery, black with red lining. At first 'FENCHURCH' was painted on one side and the company name on the other; at her repaint for her centenary 'FENCHURCH' was painted on both sides.

For the next few years *Fenchurch* was regularly in use, a valuable member of the Bluebell line's fleet. But for such a special engine, special events would undoubtedly follow. On 5th November 1972 *Fenchurch* celebrated her centenary by working two special trains, both of which comprised solely the LBSCR Directors saloon. The locomotive then received an invitation to take part in the Stockton & Darlington Railway 150th anniversary celebrations, and was among the cavalcade at Shildon on 31st August 1975. *Fenchurch* was withdrawn for overhaul soon after return from Shildon, but returned to service in August 1980. Late in 1988 she was repainted in BR lined black as No. 32636, in connection with commemoration of the 25th anniversary of the closure of the Hayling Island branch, but was withdrawn from service in May 1989, requiring major attention to the wheels.

The next 'Terrier' purchaser was rather different and somewhat unexpected. Early in 1964 it was reported that Sir Billy Butlin wanted to buy five 'Terriers' for display at his holiday camps around the country, at seaside locations. In the event, with so many other intending purchasers, he had to settle for only three 'Terriers'. These three were restored externally to a form of Stroudley LBSCR livery, but rather incongruously they retained their BR smokebox number plates. Each was displayed in company with a large LMS express locomotive.

In the early 1970s it became known that Butlins would be prepared to loan their locomotives to interested parties; this was mainly because of widespread concern that continued exposure to the sea air was not doing the locomotives any good at all. Loans of all these locomotives were arranged during the next few years, and since then most have been bought by their custodians. This has included the three 'Terriers' bought by Butlins.

The first 'Terrier' to go to Butlins was No. 32678 which left Eastleigh on 25th July 1964 and arrived at Minehead three days later. Her companion there was LMS Pacific No. 46229 *Duchess of Hamilton*. Also at Minehead, and establishing its operations there during the 1970s, was the West Somerset Railway, so it was no surprise when No. 32678 went on loan to this railway in March 1975. The 'Terrier' was stored at various places on the line, and at first no positive steps were taken towards restoration.

But in January 1980 the locomotive was purchased for £3,500 by three supporters of the West Somerset Railway. They made a start at dismantling the locomotive as the first step towards restoration, and sent the boiler away to Tavistock for specialist work to be done. However, it was decided in 1983 not to proceed with this restoration, and as the railway had no real need for a 'Terrier', the locomotive was sold in March 1983 to a director of Resco Railways, with the dismantled parts of No. 32678 leaving the West Somerset Railway on 11th April 1983.

The job of completing the restoration was then tackled at Resco's premises at Woolwich. The boiler was returned from Tavistock in 1984, with the work on

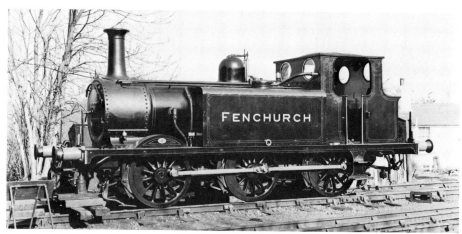

No. 32636 was restored by the Bluebell Railway as *Fenchurch*, painted in a livery based on that of the Newhaven Harbour Company. Seen at Sheffield Park on 29th April 1984.   *John Scrace*

No. 32662 was restored at Bressingham to LBSCR umber livery as No. 662. This loco has mostly been a static exhibit there, but was active on 4th August 1976, as part of her centenary celebrations.

John Scrace

it completed. The job of reconditioning other existing parts, and making new parts where necessary, continued, but in 1988 the dismantled locomotive was moved to store at the Kent & East Sussex Railway, where it is planned to complete the restoration.

Next to go to Butlins was No. 32640, which went to their Pwllheli camp late in July 1964, being seen passing Birmingham on 30th July. Her LMS companion at Pwllheli was 'Pacific' No. 46203 *Princess Margaret Rose*, and she stayed there for over eight years.

The Wight Locomotive Society was formed in 1966, and from the first pursued the preservation of items of rolling stock with historical connections with the Isle of Wight. The Society's steam railway at Havenstreet was established in 1971, and preserved items were gathered together there. So when, in the early 1970s, Butlins started to make their locomotives available, No. 32640 was soon identified as highly appropriate for the Isle of Wight Steam Railway. This locomotive had served on the island from 1902 to 1947 (the longest period of service of any 'Terrier' on the Island), and is the only surviving Isle of Wight Central Railway locomotive (and the Isle of Wight Steam Railway is a section of the old IWCR).

Following negotiations with Butlins, No. 32640 left Pwllheli on 23rd January 1973 and arrived back on the Isle of Wight four days later. She was delivered to Ryde, where it was hoped that restoration could proceed as a background job in the Works, as facilities at Havenstreet were minimal at this point. But in the event it was not possible to do very much work on the locomotive at Ryde. So, on 17th January 1975, No. 32640 was moved to Havenstreet, and now sat once more on IWCR metals. In the early months of 1975 she was restored externally to IWCR condition as No. 11 in lined black livery, with a wooden replica of a Wheeler & Hurst chimney of the Island pattern. No. 11 was officially handed over to the Wight Locomotive Society on 24th August 1975 at a ceremony which was part of the centenary celebrations of the Ryde & Newport Railway. Towards the end of 1975 it was decided to restore the locomotive to working order, and the Wight Locomotive Society bought No. 11 from Butlins for £3,500 on 4th July 1976.

Dismantling this locomotive proved to be very much more difficult than expected, owing to the effects of the long stay at Pwllheli. The dismantling process was still in progress in June 1979 when No. 32646 (W8) arrived on the Island, and was found to be in a much more readily repairable state than No. 11. Work on No. 11 continued, but slowed down appreciably, and when the new repair shop at Havenstreet came into use No. 11 was the first locomotive to go in, on 3rd January 1981.

In the more civilised setting of the repair shop, work continued steadily, though keeping other locomotives in traffic had to take precedence. As No. 11 was being restored to IWCR condition, and had lost her Drummond chimney to No. W8, a new chimney, of the Wheeler & Hurst pattern used by the IWCR, was cast using the 1975 wooden replica as a pattern. Completion

of other work led to a hydraulic test in November 1986, but this was not successful; steps were taken to correct the problem, and No. W11 was steamed for the first time on 25th June 1989, returning to service on 13th August following.

The third and last of the 'Terriers' sold to Butlins was No. 32662, which left Eastleigh for Ayr on a Flatrol on 25th September 1964. The locomotive joined the LMS Pacific No. 46233 *Duchess of Sutherland* at Ayr, and was moved to the Heads of Ayr camp on 19th October.

This 'Terrier's' exile at Heads of Ayr ended when she left the camp on 25th February 1971, and she was then moved to the Bressingham Steam Museum, near Diss in Norfolk, where she arrived in March. Her centenary was celebrated in August 1976 with the engine, restored to LBSCR umber livery as No. 662, in steam and giving footplate rides. Otherwise she has remained a static exhibit; she received a further external overhaul about 1979, remaining in umber brown as No. 662. In 1987 the remaining Butlins locomotives were offered for sale, with the existing custodians in each case having first refusal. No. 662 was the only 'Terrier' remaining in their ownership, and in May 1989 she was bought by the Bressingham Steam Museum Trust.

Finally, the two remaining 'Terriers' were purchased, to make a clean sweep of the seven withdrawn by British Railways in the latter months of 1963. Both of these two, after widely differing sequences of events, have given extensive service on the preserved lines where they are now resident.

Early in 1964 the London Borough of Sutton decided they wanted to buy a 'Terrier' to feature as a static exhibit in their new civic centre. The obvious choice was No. 32661 (ex *Sutton*) but when the Borough asked for this locomotive they found it had been cut up in September 1963; they were offered No. 32650 instead, and decided this would be an acceptable substitute. However, the Sutton civic centre was not yet ready to receive a 'Terrier', and the Kent and East Sussex Railway offered to provide a home for the locomotive in the mean time. This was not a particularly appropriate 'Terrier' for the K&ESR – of the ten survivors this was one of only three which had no record of any previous connection with the line; but really, any 'Terrier' will fit in well on the K&ESR.

No. 32650 proceeded on her delivery run from Eastleigh on 18th September 1964, stopping overnight at Eastbourne and proceeding on to Robertsbridge the next day. On her arrival there was a handover ceremony, with the Mayor of Sutton and other borough officials present. She then remained in store at Robertsbridge until used to haul carriage stock over the K&ESR line to Rolvenden at Whitsun 1966, and later that year was officially named *Sutton*; many 'Terriers' have had two names at various times – this is the only one that has had three – *Whitechapel*, *Fishbourne* and now *Sutton*.

After overhaul in 1968-69, which included repainting in K&ESR 'house' colours of lined light green, *Sutton* was in regular service from 1969 to 1972. During

Static exhibits are normally to be found in museums, but No. 32646, restored externally as No. 46 *Newington*, spent 13 years on display outside the Hayling Billy public house, where she is seen on 12th March 1967. Later she returned to the Isle of Wight as No. W8. *John Scrace*

Preserved steam locomotives sometimes have to take on strange guises for filming and similar purposes. No. 32678 has become 'No. 5' on somebody's railway, lacking a dome cover; this is at Minehead, 8th October 1979. *S.C. Nash*

this time the K&ESR remained officially closed, though various workings continued; the first official train ran on the line on 3rd February 1974 and *Sutton* was one of the two locomotives that worked it. The official reopening ceremony of the line was on 1st June 1974, and *Sutton* again participated. By this time the locomotive had become No. 10 in the K&ESR's stock, and she remained active for most of the rest of the decade. This included the cavalcade held on 25th and 26th September 1976 to celebrate this 'Terrier's' centenary.

On 1st January 1980 No. 10 was withdrawn from service for extensive repairs, and in 1981 a 30 year lease was negotiated with the Borough of Sutton, to ensure No. 10's continued presence on the line into the 21st century. *Sutton* returned to service in September 1984 in a modified light green livery. Then, after a further overhaul she returned to service on 10th April 1988 in Southern Railway 1930s lined green, but retaining the

identity of No. 10 *Sutton*. This is an interesting play on numbers and liveries - she now has the appearance of an Isle of Wight 'Terrier' (which she was) but with a number she did not carry on the Island, and with a name never carried by any Island locomotive.

The last 'Terrier' to be despatched by British Railways was No. 32646, which travelled to Droxford, on the Meon Valley line, on 28th November 1964, following sale to Mr. Charles Ashby of the Sadler Railcar Company. The locomotive remained based at Droxford for the next year and more. It was put out that she had been bought for the purpose of propelling the company's railcar (unpowered at this stage) on a section of the line, to test the railcar's riding qualities. In the event the 'Terrier' was in steam only a very few times.

About eighteen months later No. 32646 was sold again, to Brickwoods Brewery for use as an outsize sign for the 'Hayling Billy' public house on Hayling Island.

On her return to the Isle of Wight, No. 32640 was initially restored externally to IWCR condition as No. 11, with a replica of the Wheeler & Hurst pattern of chimney. The locomotive is on view at Havenstreet on 24th August 1975, during the Ryde & Newport Railway centenary celebrations. *John Goss*

The sale and departure to Hayling were marked by a special working on 13th May 1966. No. 32646 was steamed and worked a former Southern Railway restaurant car, containing directors of the brewery company and their guests, down the Meon Valley line through Wickham to Knowle Halt, and back. Four days later No. 32646 was moved by low loader to Hayling Island and installed on a short stretch of track outside the 'Hayling Billy' public house. The LBSCR yellow livery was restored, and the locomotive became No. 46 *Newington* once more. She remained outside the pub for the next thirteen years, and most people assumed she had steamed her last.

By the late 1970s, several groups had decided that *Newington* would make a fine addition to the stock of the steam railway of their choice, and had accordingly approached Whitbread Wessex Ltd, who had taken over Brickwood in the meantime. One such group was the Wight Locomotive Society, who had the distinct advantage that the locomotive had strong connections with the Isle of Wight; indeed, she had one of the longest spells of service on the Island of any 'Terrier', exceeded only by No. W11 and (by a very small margin) by the late No. W10. The Society were able to press their claim to a successful conclusion, and in June 1979 the locomotive was donated to them. Even while still outside the pub, *Newington* was repainted in SR lined green as No. W8, and she left Hayling Island on 18th June 1979. She arrived at Havenstreet on 25th June and on 9th August was officially handed over, the ceremonies including the restoration of her old island name *Freshwater*.

The Wight Locomotive Society soon discovered that despite all those years outside the pub, they now had a far more restorable 'Terrier' than No. 11 (32640) with which they had been wrestling for over three years. Work proceeded rapidly enough for trial steamings of No. W8 to take place in August 1980, and after further repairs the locomotive returned to service on 21st June 1981. The Drummond chimney from No. 11 had been fitted, as No. W8's Stroudley chimney was no longer useable, so the locomotive's condition in the mid 1930s is now recreated.

Since her return to traffic No. W8 has borne the brunt of the traffic on the line, and apart from a spell in 1986 has remained almost continuously available for service. In 1989 the locomotive was repainted in FYNR livery as their No. 2, as part of the celebrations of the centenary of the opening of the FYNR.

This generous representation of the 'Terrier' class in preservation means that a full range of variants can be seen. There are 'Terriers' with Stroudley, Marsh and Drummond chimneys, with large and small bunkers (with and without coal rails), etc., etc. – just about all the varieties one could ask for. Livery is a potentially changeable matter, but here too we have seen LBSCR, SR and BR styles, plus a few freelance essays. Their stories in preservation provide a variety almost the equal of their earlier histories – a pub sign, static exhibits at holiday camps, a 'Terrier' in Canada, etc. In preservation the 'Terriers' do indeed remain a considerable phenomenon.

A really rural railway. The Isle of Wight Steam Railway runs through pleasant woodlands, where No. W8 *Freshwater* (former BR No. 32646) is seen at work on 7th May 1984. The locomotive has been fitted with the Drummond chimney formerly carried by No. 32640. *Mike Esau*

'Terriers' in tandem. *Above:* The Bluebell Railway's *Fenchurch* and *Stepney* at work in the mid-1980s, on a slightly 'mixed' train. *Below:* the Kent & East Sussex Railway's No. 10 *Sutton* (BR No. 32650), and No. 32670 (No. 3 *Bodiam*) on an even more mixed train, on 20th October 1985.

Mike Esau

The one hundredth Stroudley locomotive. Over 25 years after entering service, No. 110 *Burgundy* is still in largely original condition, with copper-capped chimney, Stroudley dome, and goods green livery. The 'E1' is at Three Bridges, its home base for many years, in April 1903.
F. Burtt collection, National Railway Museum, York

Probably about ten years later, and still not much change. The name is gone, the livery is Marsh style and coal rails have been fitted to the bunker. The brake shoes are much smaller, so wood has presumably given way to steel. The meat merchant's display board on the nearby building suggests the location is Hove, during one of the loco's rare spells away from Three Bridges.
Lens of Sutton

'E' Class No. 110 *Burgundy*

A fair part of Stroudley's fame and reputation derives from the three highly successful classes of tank locomotive he designed for the LBSCR. The 'Terriers' were the first of these three classes, but the other two were distinctly bigger engines. The second Stroudley tank design was the 'D' class 0-4-2 tank of 1873, of which 125 were built, making it the most numerous class built by any part of the Southern Railway; it was a simple, compact, rugged design which found use all over the LBSCR system, mostly on passenger workings.

The third Stroudley tank design was the 'E' class of 1874, a 0-6-0 tank locomotive for short range goods and general shunting work. The design was clearly related to the 'D' class, used the same pattern of boiler, and had other parts in common. Stroudley built 72 of the 'E' class, Nos. 85-156, between 1874 and 1883, and his successor R.J. Billinton built six more with some modifications. Like the 'Terriers', the 'E' class were mostly built in batches of six, and No. 110 *Burgundy* was the second engine of the third batch, and thus the fourteenth engine in the class; more significantly, No. 110 was the one hundredth Stroudley engine, and this was celebrated by a dinner at the Royal Pavilion, Brighton, where the toast 'the hundredth engine' was drunk in Burgundy wine by Stroudley and some of his senior works staff.

No. 110 was completed at Brighton in March 1877 and was initially based at Brighton; about 1889 the locomotive was transferred to Three Bridges, and this remained her base almost throughout her working career with the LBSCR and Southern. Only occasionally and briefly was No. 110 recorded based elsewhere, mostly at Brighton. In due course she received Marsh livery and lost the name, and in December 1907 she was transferred to the duplicate list, being assigned a nominal value of £125 in 1911. But mechanically No. 110 changed hardly at all, and reached the 1923 Grouping still the complete Stroudley locomotive, with a copper capped chimney and a genuine Stroudley boiler.

Withdrawals of the 'E' class, by now known as the 'E1' class, had begun in 1908, with a batch of them going in 1913, but 63 of them entered Southern Railway service. Withdrawals began again in 1925, and in February 1927 No. 110 was withdrawn, still in Stroudley condition and in LBSCR livery. The locomotive was recorded as sold on 5th April 1927 to Messrs Cohens for £925, which contrasts with the 1911 nominal value of £125. She was clearly resold almost immediately, the new owners being the Cannock and Rugeley Colliery Company. They altered the locomotive fairly radically in 1929 by fitting a new boiler, made by Bagnalls of Stafford and of 'free lance' design, a tapered chimney and small cab side windows; the chimney was standard for the colliery company's locomotives, but did not sit very well on a Stroudley locomotive. No. 110 became CRC No. 9 *Cannock Wood* and carried metal insignia of ownership, number and name.

The Cannock & Rugeley Colliery's railway system comprised a 5 mile line from Hednesford to Rawnsley (the Cannock Chase branch) and a parallel line, the Littleworth Tramway. These two lines came together at Rawnsley, where they had an end-on junction with the Cannock Chase and Wolverhampton Railway, which ran from Rawnsley to Anglesey Basin. No. 9, like most CRC locomotives, operated over all these lines, and was mostly employed on colliery trip working, plus regular use on workmen's trains.

No. 110 was a comparatively early withdrawal among the 'E1' class, of which 48 still remained in service on the Southern. A small number more were withdrawn in the next decade, and four of these were sold to various other collieries around the country, following the pattern set by No. 110; like No. 110 they all appear to have given good service over a long period. On the Southern Railway the class continued to serve as shunters, mostly of course on the old LBSCR system, but also found work in certain other areas; this proved a distinct versatility and general usefulness, though most of them were around 50 years old by this time.

In the late 1920s a need arose for a small tank engine for local goods and other workings in the West

---

Dimensions

Wheel arrangement	0-6-0
Cylinders (2) – bore	17"
stroke	24"
Driving wheel diameter	4'6"
Boiler pressure	175 lb/sq.in
Tractive effort	19,106 lbs
Wheelbase	15' 3"
Overall length	32'4½"
Overall height	12'4⅛"
Weight in working order	44 tons 3 cwt
Water capacity	900 gallons
Coal capacity	1¾ tons

Stephenson link motion, slide valves, lever reverse, left hand drive

(Boiler details are not given, as a non-LBSCR boiler is carried)

Service History

Type introduced – October 1874

No. 110

Built by – LBSCR, Brighton (duplicate list 12/07)
Cost – £2800
Service date – March 1877
Numbers:-   LBSCR   – 110 (3/77)
                      CRC   – 9 (4/27)
Withdrawn ... May 1963   Final mileage ...... unknown*
          (approx.)

* No. 110 had run 998,698 miles at the Grouping in 1923, but no later figures are available.

No. 110 is now in the last year of main line service, and remains outwardly as ever. The copper capped chimney and condensing pipes remain, as the locomotive lurks in the recesses of Brighton shed, on 3rd July 1926. *H.C. Casserley*

A substantial transformation. The new boiler, with a quite different pattern of dome, is bigger than before and has pushed the side tanks out across the running plate. Side windows have been cut in the cab and a whistle is perched on the cab roof. With new, incongruous, chimney, No. 110 has become No. 9 *Cannock Wood* of the Cannock & Rugeley Colliery Co. *Author's collection*

This is how No. 110 would probably have looked in later days, if she had remained in SR and BR ownership. A number of 'E1s' received LSWR pattern chimneys, and BR unlined black was standard. No. 32113, at Eastleigh in the early 1950s, was from the same 1877 batch as No. 110. *Photomatic*

Country section of the Southern, west of Exeter. Ten of the remaining 'E1s' were modified by fitting a much larger bunker and a trailing pony truck. In this form they became the 'E1R' class 0-6-2 tanks, which served on assorted local duties around Torrington, and later became regulars on the Exeter St. Davids-to-Central banking duties. They were withdrawn from this work between 1955 and 1959.

A second unexpected area of 'E1' work was on the Isle of Wight. In the early 1930s, with the 'O2s' well established on the main Island passenger workings, and 'Terriers' on certain branch duties, the 'E1' class was identified as suitable for the small number of freight duties on the Island. Four 'E1s' were despatched to the Island in 1932 and 1933, having been refurbished and fitted with LSWR Drummond chimneys (that item of 1930s Isle of Wight locomotive uniform). As Nos. W1-W4, named (of course), these 'E1s' handled the Island goods work until the duties tailed off in the 1950s, and they were withdrawn between 1956 and 1960.

Back on the mainland, 'E1s' continued to find various shunting and similar niches through the 1930s and 1940s, with their numbers gradually dwindling. One area where they were adopted fairly late in the day was Southampton Docks; they first appeared there during the Second World War. This was eventually to be the workplace of the last mainland 'E1s', and the very last, No. 32694 (LBSCR No. 102 of 1875) was withdrawn in July 1961.

But Cannock and Rugeley Colliery No. 9 outlasted all of these in service, and was withdrawn around May 1963, the last active 'E1' anywhere. For many years No. 9 had been a well liked and well used locomotive on the CRC's railway, but was later involved in two fatal accidents, and acquired a 'jinx' among the local staff. Because of this it is alleged the locomotive's firebox was sabotaged around the time of withdrawal, to prevent preservation.

Rolling home – the day's work is done and No. 9 *Cannock Wood* passes Cannock Wood on her way back to base, on 9th September 1958.
P.J. Shoesmith

In Preservation

The 'E1' class was introduced only about two years after the 'Terriers', and so had an almost equal historical claim to fame. But in practice they came to be widely regarded as just another class of 0-6-0 tank engine, even if a very old one. The Bluebell Railway in its earliest years appreciated their historic value and the last 'E1' in BR service, No. 32694, was included in one of the early Bluebell short lists of candidates for preservation, but no purchase was effected. The last 'E1' on the Isle of Wight likewise evaded preservation.

Then, with the cause apparently lost, it was discovered that CRC No. 9 had been withdrawn around May 1963, and remained in store at the colliery's depot at Rawnsley; all thoughts of restoration to authentic Stroudley form could be rapidly dispelled, though, as the locomotive's modifications since purchase had been considerable. Soon after withdrawal, CRC No. 9 was bought by the Railway Preservation Society (Midland Area) and moved to their depot at Hednesford in December 1963. There the 'E1' received some external attention, and was then moved to the Society's line at Chasewater in May 1970. No. 9 received little attention at Chasewater, and on finding the extent of the work needed for restoration, the Society decided to sell her. The sabotage to the firebox seemed to be having the intended effect. She was bought by three supporters of the East Somerset Railway and was moved to their depot at Cranmore in September 1978.

The 'E1' was stored at Cranmore until early in 1986 when restoration work began; up to then the most noticeable job that had been done was to replace the CRC chimney with one of LSWR Drummond pattern, such as a number of 'E1s' had carried in their later days in service. Extensive repairs were put in hand, but the work needed on the boiler was found to require considerable expenditure. The boiler was eventually returned from contractors at the end of October 1989, with the work on it complete; other tasks were then being tackled, with the prospect of return to running order in the near future.

Thoughts of preservation are clearly in the air, as the withdrawn No. 9 sits at Hednesford in the 1960s, between a couple of vintage carriages. By this time No. 9 had been recognised as an item of much historical worth, but the cost of repairs inhibited restoration for many years.   *R.C. Riley*

Eventually the Chasewater Railway, No. 9's first owners in preservation, decided they could not really afford the cost of putting the engine into running order. So they sold her to the East Somerset Railway, where she is seen on 16th August 1981. The Drummond chimney fitted at this point is certainly authentic for the class, though not for this locomotive, while the number 32110, and the 82H shedplate, are entirely figments of someone's imagination.

J.A. McMillen

'B' Class No. 214 *Gladstone*

Stroudley's first express engines were a small class of 2-4-0s, which made use of some existing parts; they were followed by a series of 2-2-2s which were entirely his own design and quite characteristic, though following the practice of the time. His final express passenger design, however, was unique among the express locomotives of its day. The starting point was the 'D' class 0-4-2 tank design. From this Stroudley developed the 'D2' or 'Lyons' class 0-4-2 mixed traffic tender engines of 1876. The next step was the 'Richmond' class 0-4-2 express design of 1878, and from this he developed the final 'Gladstone' class 0-4-2. The use of large front-coupled wheels on an express locomotive was very unusual, and was regarded with great misgiving in many quarters at the time, with widespread prophecies of disaster when such locomotives were used in everyday traffic. Many were sure that the first encounter with any sort of complicated trackwork at speed would inevitably cause immediate derailment. Stroudley maintained this mechanical layout was perfectly stable, and the locomotives in practice proved him correct.

In the early years the 'Richmonds' and 'Gladstones' were grouped together in the 'B' class, but the 'Gladstones' became the 'B1' class in Marsh's time. No. 214 *Gladstone* was the first engine of its type, and was turned out of Brighton Works on the last day of 1882. She was, of course, painted in full Stroudley passenger livery and was initially based at Brighton; indeed, throughout her career there is little evidence of this locomotive ever being based anywhere else. 36 'Gladstones' were constructed between 1882 and 1891, and they were numbered 172-200 and 214-220. The 0-4-2 layout made possible a very compact locomotive, which was able to fit on the LBSCR's rather small turntables.

The 'Gladstones' were used from the start on prime express workings, principally on London-Brighton expresses. Stroudley continued to turn these engines out up to the time of his death, and so left unanswered the question of how he could develop a more powerful design from the 'Gladstone' type, which did not appear to lend itself to further development. The 'B2' class, R.J. Billinton's first express design, had the 4-4-0 wheel arrangement that was in widespread use by the 1890s, but they were under-boilered and did not displace the 'Gladstones' from the best passenger turns; however, in 1899 Billinton introduced the much larger 'B4' class 4-4-0s, which did start to supersede the 'Gladstones', and the 0-4-2s began to move to secondary duties.

No. 214 *Gladstone* was largely unaltered structurally during R.J. Billinton's term of office, but his successor D.E. Marsh brought in some changes. Most of the 'B1' class (as they now became) lost their names in Marsh's time, though *Gladstone* was already a sufficiently celebrated locomotive to be treated as a special case, and retained the name; this was still painted on the splashers, but on the new livery of umber brown. Marsh soon began to fit the 'B1' class with new boilers, of his own revised design; *Gladstone* was one of the first to receive such a boiler, in 1907, and ran with a sequence of Marsh boilers until withdrawal. Stroudley's original design of boiler had, following his normal practice, safety valves with spring balances, mounted in the dome, which was on the third ring of the boiler; Marsh's usual pattern of boiler, which he followed in reboilering the Gladstones, had separate safety valves above the firebox, and the dome on the second ring. At first *Gladstone* retained the Stroudley copper capped chimney, but just before the Grouping of 1923 this was replaced by the Marsh pattern.

Dimensions

Wheel arrangement	0-4-2
Cylinders (2) – bore	18¾"
stroke	26"
Driving wheel diameter	6'6"
Boiler pressure	160 lb/sq.in
Tractive effort	15,100 lbs
Wheelbase	15' 7"
Overall length	51' 8½"
Overall height	13' 3½"

Weight in working order	68 tons 1 cwt
Grate area	20.3 sq.ft
Total heating surface	1351 sq.ft
Boiler tubes	276 x 1⅝"
Water capacity	2238 gallons
Coal capacity	4 tons

Stephenson link motion, slide valves, screw reverse, left hand drive

Service History

Type introduced – December 1882

No. 214

Built by – LBSCR, Brighton (duplicate list 12/09)
Cost – £2655
Service date – December 1882
Numbers:-

	LBSCR	– 214 (12/82), 618 (6/20)
	SR	– B618 (9/24)

Withdrawn . . . April 1927   Final mileage 1,346,918

Here is No. 214 *Gladstone*, little altered from original condition. The only obvious change is that a continuous handrail has been fitted. The dome (and its position) tell us that a Stroudley pattern boiler is fitted, and the original very short smokebox door hinge arms are in place.

Lens of Sutton

Variations in the reboilering of *Gladstone*.

Left: A Marsh boiler has been fitted, with relatively tall dome cover and plain safety valve cover, while the cabside number is still carried on a plate.

Author's collection

Below: This must be after at least one further reboilering – a shorter dome cover, ornate safety valve cover, and the cabside numerals are painted. The location is St Leonards.

F. Burtt collection, National Railway Museum, York

Variations of smokebox door hinges, boiler washout plugs, etc, can also be detected in these and the other photographs.

The only preserved LBSCR express passenger locomotive is seen at work on main line passenger duties. These are latter-day views of *Gladstone*, so the locomotive is no longer working prime express duties.

Above: Gladstone on the Brighton main line – No. 214 approaches Purley on an up train in July 1911; cabside numberplate and relatively tall dome.

W.L. Kenning

Below: Gladstone was renumbered 618 in 1920, and is seen on a Portsmouth-Brighton train near Barnham Junction, the same year.

H. Gordon Tidey

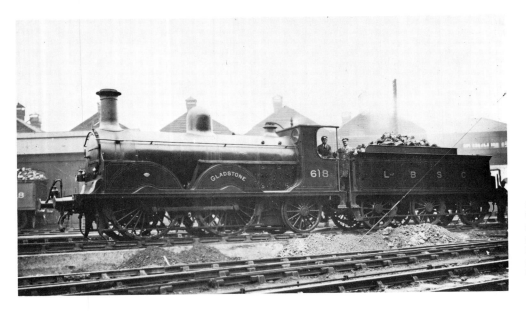

Gladstone in final LBSCR form – the locomotive received a Marsh chimney not long after being re-numbered 618. Coping has been fitted to the tender, and this shot must be around the time of the Grouping. *H. Gordon Tidey*

In Marsh's time newer locomotives, including his 'Atlantics' and 'I3' class tanks, had pushed the 'Gladstones' even further down the scale, and the first withdrawals of the type took place in 1910, as the older boilers were wearing out and were not considered worth refurbishing. *Gladstone* had regularly averaged around 40,000 miles per year until 1905, and only a bit less than this up to 1910, but after that the annual figure fell right away to around 15,000 miles per year. This reflected *Gladstone's* changed employment by this time, as the earlier regular work on London-Brighton expresses had now given place to secondary workings from Brighton along the coast, westward to Portsmouth and eastward to Hastings.

Gladstone's diminishing status was reflected in other ways, too. At the end of 1909 the locomotive was placed on the duplicate list, and in July 1920 she was renumbered 618, as part of a process to free some numbers for new construction. On becoming Southern Railway property the locomotive lost her name and became SR No. B618, in Southern lined green passenger livery, in September 1924.

26 of the 36 'Gladstones' had entered Southern Railway stock, but withdrawals began again in earnest in 1925, when it became apparent there was little work available for them on the Southern of the 1920s. The former *Gladstone* (No. B618) went soon after this, being officially withdrawn in April 1927; eighteen of the class remained in service at this point, but they all departed in the next few years. The last survivor was No. B172, withdrawn in September 1933.

This is the final running state of *Gladstone*, ex-works after the final general overhaul at Brighton in September 1924. The loco is now Southern Railway No. B618, and the name has finally gone; there is no cabside number plate, as Brighton did not start to fit these until around May 1925.

A.B. MacLeod

In Preservation

The preservation of *Gladstone* was a very remarkable and historic achievement indeed. In 1927 this was the first British locomotive to be preserved privately. Sixty years later the private preservation of a locomotive, by a society or a group of individuals, is considered commonplace; *Gladstone* was the first. It is a measure of Stroudley's lasting reputation that one of his locomotives should have been the subject of this pioneering operation.

Gladstone was donated to the Stephenson Locomotive Society (SLS) by the Southern Railway in December 1926; the SR's General Manager reported this to the railway's Locomotive Committee on 26th January 1927, saying that the SLS had requested that 'one of the late Mr William Stroudley's locomotives should be preserved as a permanent record' and adding that *Gladstone*, then due for breaking up, was the most suitable. The SLS agreed to pay the £140 estimated cost of restoring the locomotive to original condition, including painting; the plan was that the locomotive would then be placed in the Science Museum. But the Science Museum did not have room to take *Gladstone*, so the locomotive was then offered to the York Queen Street Railway Museum on an interim basis. The York museum said they would be happy to take *Gladstone*, but only for a longer term, with a guarantee of at least a ten year stay.

This was agreed, and during the early months of 1927 restoration was carried out at Brighton. A boiler in the Stroudley manner (but actually from R.J. Billinton's time) replaced *Gladstone's* final Marsh boiler,

a copper capped chimney was fitted, the original discontinuous hand rail arrangement was reinstated, and the Stroudley livery was restored. All this was completed around the middle of May 1927; *Gladstone* was then briefly on display in London before being hauled north, and arrived at York on 27th May, being placed in the museum on 28th, with the official handover ceremony on 31st. The York museum had up to then concerned itself principally with LNER items, and *Gladstone* was their first 'foreign' locomotive, though not their first 'foreign' item of any sort, as one of the Bodmin and Wadebridge Railway carriages had arrived the previous year.

Since 1927, as a static museum exhibit, *Gladstone's* life has been relatively uneventful. She stayed in the York museum through the 1930s, but was sent to Reedsmouth in 1941 for wartime storage, returning after the end of the war. *Gladstone* remained in the ownership of the Stephenson Locomotive Society until presented to the British Transport Commission on 18th September 1959; the society had found that the locomotive needed a repaint, and this they could not afford, so she was handed over to a larger body who could.

Gladstone remained in the Queen Street museum until its closure in 1974. She was then transferred the short distance to the new National Railway Museum, situated the other side of York station, and was on display there when the new museum opened in September 1975. The next celebration was in 1977, the jubilee of *Gladstone's* original preservation, when a further thorough refurbishment was carried out.

In the restoration of *Gladstone* in 1927 the clock was put well and truly back. A Stroudley pattern boiler was fitted, with a copper capped chimney, and discontinuous handrails. The coping was removed from the tender sides, and shorter smokebox door hinge arms were fitted, though not as short as the original pattern. With the Stroudley livery restored, No. 214 was extensively photographed at Battersea Park and elsewhere in London before proceeding to York. Seen at Battersea Park, 21st May 1927.
H.C. Casserley

For the next forty years and more *Gladstone* was resident at the old York Queen Street Museum, apart from a period of wartime storage. Here, far from her native haunts, she was mostly in the company of locomotives of the LNER constituent companies, such as (here) the Stirling 8ft Single No. 1. *Author's collection*

Apart from the wartime evacuation, *Gladstone* had remained continuously resident at York since preservation. Then in 1982 the locomotive travelled south to former haunts, arriving at the Bluebell Railway on 24th March and staying through the summer to participate in the centenary celebrations of the East Grinstead-Culver Junction line (of which the Bluebell is part) on 31st July and 1st August 1982. This was a double centenary, as it was also the 100th anniversary of *Gladstone's* construction, and it was fitting that *Gladstone* and the Bluebell Railway, both pioneers in their respective fields of preservation, should celebrate it together. *Gladstone* returned to York in the autumn and has remained there since. The NRM at York is part of the Science Museum – so, in a way, the original plan for *Gladstone's* residence in retirement has finally been achieved.

Finally, Gladstone travelled south again in 1982 to take part in the Bluebell Railway's celebrations for the centenary of the original opening of their line. She is seen at Sheffield Park on 11th July 1982. *John Scrace*

'E4' Class No. 473 *Birch Grove*

Stroudley's last design for the LBSCR was the 0-6-2 tank locomotive No. 158 *West Brighton*, a development of the 'E1' class and his only locomotive on eight wheels. After some delay, this locomotive was completed by R.J. Billinton in 1891, and came to form the basis of an extensive family of 0-6-2 tank locomotives built by Billinton, which became known as the Billinton Radials. These formed a major part of the LBSCR scene for over fifty years and handled work which ranged over a wide spectrum. The first of the four classes was the 'E3' class of 1894, which closely resembled *West Brighton* and into which this locomotive was eventually incorporated. The 'E3' class had 4ft 6in driving wheels and were principally intended for short distance goods workings; only sixteen 'E3s' were built (plus *West Brighton*) as it became evident that slightly larger driving wheels would give a more generally useful engine. So the second class of Billinton Radial was introduced, the 'E4' class of 1897, similar to the 'E3' class but with 5ft driving wheels and intended to handle some local passenger workings as well as local goods. This was the most numerous of the Billinton radial classes, numbering 75 in all. In the third of Billinton's classes of radial tanks the driving wheel size was further increased to 5ft 6in to produce the 'E5' class of 1902, which were used for assorted passenger workings; 30 'E5s' were built. The final design was the 'E6' class of 1904, with 4ft 6in driving wheels for heavy shunting and local goods, and twelve of these were built.

The 'E4' class were built between 1897 and 1903. No. 473 *Birch Grove* was the eleventh locomotive in the class and was completed at Brighton in June 1898, being recorded as '6 wheels coupled goods tank' of class 'E special'. The locomotive was initially allocated to New Cross and was painted in goods green livery, as were all the engines in the early batches, to show their intended use. The earlier (goods) batches of the 'E4' class had lever reverse, considered appropriate for goods work and shunting, while the later (supposedly passenger) batches were turned out in yellow ochre and with screw reverse. No. 473, like most of the 'goods' E4s', was later repainted in passenger yellow. The 'E4' class did well on secondary goods and local passenger workings in their early years, but were not sufficiently free running for any sort of main line passenger working.

The 'E4s' were originally built with boilers in the Stroudley manner, with safety valves mounted in the dome with spring balances, and with the smokebox and its saddle integral. Modifications began in the Marsh era. In September 1912 No. 473 was one of the first 'E4s' to be rebuilt with an 'I1' pattern boiler, with safety valves above the firebox and with a circular section smokebox mounted on a separate saddle; a chimney of Marsh's pattern was also fitted. A year or two before this (probably in 1909) No. 473 had received Marsh's umber livery and her name was painted out.

No. 473 remained based at New Cross for some years, though briefly at Croydon about 1908, but was transferred to Brighton about 1916 where she remained (apart from a brief stay at Newhaven) until the time of the Grouping in 1923. Under Southern Railway ownership, this locomotive was one of the first of the 'E4' class to be painted in Southern lined green passenger livery, and was renumbered B473 in February 1924. She was further renumbered 2473 in December 1932.

The 'E4' class were maintained at Ashford from about 1932, and showed evidence of Ashford practice in some of their fittings. Some of them received SECR pattern smokebox doors and safety valves, but No. 2473 seems to have kept a Brighton appearance throughout,

Dimensions

Wheel arrangement	0-6-2
Cylinders (2) – bore	17½"
stroke	26"
Driving wheel diameter	5'0"
Boiler pressure	170 lb/sq.in
Tractive effort	19,176 lbs
Wheelbase	21' 6"
Overall length	35' 3"
Overall height	12' 8⅜"

Weight in working order	56 tons 15 cwt
Grate area	17.35 sq.ft
Total heating surface	1038 sq.ft
Boiler tubes	191 x 1¾"
Water capacity	1408 gallons
Coal capacity	2½ tons

Stephenson link motion, slide valves, lever reverse, left hand drive

Service History

Type introduced – December 1897

No. 473

Built by – LBSCR, Brighton
Cost – £2219
Service date – June 1898
Numbers:-

	LBSCR	– 473 (6/98)
	SR	– B473 (2/24), 2473 (12/32)
	BR	– S2473 (2/48), 32473 (4/51)
Withdrawn ... Oct. 1962	Final mileage 1,203,967	

Left: 'E4' class No. 473 *Birch Grove*, as originally built, had the usual R.J. Billinton features – notably his characteristic tapering chimney and the smokebox with integral saddle. The locomotive retains the original pattern of boiler, with spring balance safety valves, but has been repainted yellow in place of the original green; so it is probably about 1905, at New Cross. *Bluebell RPS archives*

Above: No. 473 was one of the first 'E4s' to receive Southern Railway livery, and this is probably the occasion for this photograph. The engine is much changed – a Marsh chimney with smokebox on a separate saddle, and a boiler with separate safety valves above the firebox. The name has long since gone, and this is now No. B473.
F. Burtt collection, National Railway Museum, York

Left: After being one of the first 'E4s' to have the Southern Railway 'B' prefix, this loco was one of the few to carry the interim 'S' prefix in the early days of British Railways. No. S2473, in wartime unlined black, is at Norwood Junction shed in 1948. *R.C. Riley*

The 'E4' is now BR No. 32473 and is seen at Brighton on 21st March 1958, in lined black with the first pattern of BR crest. She has just completed a heavy intermediate overhaul in the Works; this was the last intermediate overhaul of an LBSCR locomotive at Brighton.   *J.R. Besley*

and certainly retained it at withdrawal. No. B473 was recorded as based at New Cross in 1928, and was one of fourteen 'E4s' there at the start of 1933; she had moved to Bricklayers Arms by late 1934, and then went on to Brighton in May 1935, staying there until the war.

By the end of the war No. 2473 was in the wartime black Southern livery, with sunshine lettering, and was based at Norwood Junction. This was a depot with almost entirely goods duties, so No. 2473's work would have been shunting and some local freight; any sort of passenger work would have been very rare. Indeed, by this time the 'E4' class were mainly employed on shunting, piloting and other such jobs.

In February 1948, following nationalisation, the locomotive acquired the interim 'S' prefix as No. S2473, but became BR No. 32473 in April 1951; lined black livery was applied in April 1954, with the first pattern of BR crest. In the meantime, the locomotive had been transferred to Bricklayers Arms in October 1950, with much the same range of duties as before, and she stayed there for almost a decade. By then steam was in full retreat in those parts; the locomotive received her final general repair, and the second pattern of BR crest, in June 1960 and was then transferred to Nine Elms, where she was mostly employed on carriage piloting and empty stock workings. Withdrawals of the class began on a serious scale in the late 1950s, and by 1960 over half of them were gone. By the time of No. 32473's withdrawal in October 1962 the class was down to penny numbers, and the last survivor, No. 32479, was withdrawn in June 1963.

No. 32473's final base was at Nine Elms, and this is where she is seen, early in the 1960s. This is clearly very soon after her final general overhaul and repaint in June 1960.
K.O'B. Nichols

In Preservation

The 'E4' class had been described as one of the most versatile and reliable classes of locomotive the Brighton ever possessed. They were Robert Billinton's most numerous class, and gave good service all over the LBSCR system for over half a century.

In its very earliest years the Bluebell Railway gave much thought to preservation policies. It should be remembered that this was a time when the last survivors of several historic types were still in BR service, and hardly anyone else (apart from those organising the National Collection) was concerning themselves with methodical preservation. In mid 1961 the Bluebell published their first list of locomotives which they felt were strong candidates for preservation, and a Billinton radial tank, which might be either an 'E4' or an 'E6', was included in this list. The relative merits of these two types, of which the last few of each were then in service, were discussed over the months following; the 'E6' class still remained in almost their original exterior outline, which was a significant point in their favour, but it was considered that an 'E4' would probably be more generally useful, and was likely to be more successful on passenger work.

A year later a revised list of candidates for preservation was headed by 'E4' class No. 32473. This had, in the meantime, been identified as one of the best of the small band of survivors, and was then, rather fortuitously, found to have originally carried the name *Birch Grove*, which was an estate close to the Bluebell line and the home of the Prime Minister at that time, Harold Macmillan.

No. 32473 was purchased direct from BR service at Nine Elms for around £850, and arrived on the Bluebell Railway on 16th October 1962. She was soon in use, in 'as delivered' condition, but at the same time her permanent livery was discussed. Her original livery was inappropriate to the locomotive as preserved, so it was decided to use Marsh umber brown, and then, taking a bit of a liberty with strict historical authenticity, to reinstate the name *Birch Grove* on this livery. This livery and name were restored in the spring of 1963.

Birch Grove was in service on the Bluebell Railway from this point, with only short breaks for repairs, until 1971. She was then withdrawn from service, requiring a full overhaul. Some work was done during 1983-85, but this was then suspended; it is hoped that work can resume shortly.

The preserved 'E4' has been restored at the Bluebell Railway as No. 473 *Birch Grove*, painted in LBSCR umber brown. Here she is seen at work on the line on 20th September 1970. *Mike Esau*

Boilers

Of the thirteen preserved LBSCR locomotives, only one carries a boiler from the same period as the locomotive itself. Most of the others carry replacement boilers dating from the early decades of the 20th century, and one even carries a boiler of completely non-Brighton origin.

The LBSCR numbered all its boilers in ascending sequence starting from the beginning of the Stroudley era, and this included boilers built for the railway by outside firms. Except where indicated otherwise, all these surviving boilers were built at Brighton.

'A' Class No. 82

Boxhill carries the boiler, No. 194, with which the locomotive was built in 1880, and there is no evidence that locomotive and boiler have ever been separated.

'A1X' Class

The 'A1X' pattern of boiler was introduced in 1911 to reboiler the 'Terriers', when their success at motor train working indicated there would be work for them to do for some years yet. Over the next decade or so, these boilers were fitted to most of the remaining active 'Terriers' on the LBSCR, and also to a few previously sold out of service to other companies. A rebuild to 'A1X' included fitting an extended smokebox, but two 'Terriers' received 'A1X' boilers without the extended smokebox, and remained classified 'A1' rather than 'A1X' (and one 'A1X' ended its days fitted with a Stroudley boiler).

Twenty-one 'A1X' boilers were built, and of these nine survive on preserved 'Terriers'. These nine range from boiler No. 935, one of the original pair of 1911, to No. 1237, almost the last built, and they include two which were renumbered by Eastleigh around 1930; these were Nos. 935 and 986, which were renumbered 553 and 1008 respectively, to avoid clashes with existing Eastleigh boiler numbers.

Loco No. 50 (K&ESR No. 10) now has boiler No. 935, renumbered 553 in 1930, of which the history is:-
New on No. 678 (11/11), to No. E735 (5/30), to No. 680S (2/37), to No. 32677 (9/52), to No. 32636 (10/57), to No. 32650 (3/63)

No. 40 (IWCR No. 11) has boiler No. 967:-
New on No. 653 (5/12), to No. 2678 (7/37), to No. 32661 (2/54), to No. 32640 (11/58)

No. 54 (BR No. DS680) has boiler No. 986, which was renumbered 1008 in 1930:-
New on No. 655 (10/12), to No. B662 (11/27), to No. W9 (5/30), to No. DS680 (5/52)

No. 46 (SR No. W8) has boiler No. 1012:-
New on *Fenchurch* (4/13), to No. 32646 (2/58)

No. 72 (*Fenchurch*) has boiler No. 1014:-
New on No. 663 (5/13), to No. W11 (4/27), to No. W8 (12/37), to No. DS515 (2/52), to No. 32677 (8/57), to No. 32636 (3/62)

No. 70 (K&ESR No. 3) has boiler No. 1032:-
New on No. 662 (12/13), to No. B661 (9/28), to No. 2655 (12/39), to No. 32678 (7/53), to No. 32670 (5/60)

No. 78 has boiler No. 1128:-
New on No. 650 (5/20), to No. W13 (5/32), to No. 32655 (4/53), to No. 32678 (9/59)

No. 62 has boiler No. 1172:-
New on No. 635 (4/22), to No. 2661 (4/39), to No. 32670 (3/54), to No. 32662 (3/61)

No. 55 has boiler No. 1237:-
New on No. B655 (1/27), to K&ESR No. 3 (3/44), to No. 32662 (9/49), to No. 32640 (2/56), to No. 32655 (6/59)

'E' Class No. 110

No. 110 retained a Stroudley boiler throughout its service on the LBSCR, being reboilered in 1893, 1901 and 1914, and receiving a Stroudley boiler in each case. However, shortly after sale to the Cannock & Rugeley Colliery Co. Ltd a replacement boiler built by Bagnalls (works No. 7496) was fitted, and this has no claim to LBSCR authenticity.

'B' Class No. 214

Gladstone retained its original boiler until 1902, when it received another Stroudley boiler. But in 1907 it received a new boiler of Marsh pattern, and further varieties of this pattern at reboilerings in 1912, 1913, 1920 and 1924. Following withdrawal, as part of the restoration of the locomotive, Stroudley pattern boiler No. 732 was fitted. This was built by the Vulcan Foundry, and its history is:-

New on No. 185 (5/01), to No. 177 (10/08), to No. 214 (4/27)

'E4' Class No. 473

By chance, this locomotive now carries the very boiler that was fitted new to it when it was reboilered by Marsh. This is boiler No. 981, of which the history is:-

New on 'E4' No. 473 (9/12), to 'D3' No. 373 (7/20), to 'D3' No. 365 (7/21), to 'D3' No. 376 (3/28), to 'D3' No. 2389 (11/34), to 'D3' No. 2374 (6/40), to 'D3' No. 2377 (2/44), to 'E3' No. 32458 (9/49), to 'E3' No. 32166 (4/52), to 'E4' No. 32473 (6/60)

Preserved LBSCR Carriages

All drawings to 4mm scale

Five carriages of LBSCR origin are preserved, and all of them were bought from British Railways in the 1960s. In addition, a number of LBSCR grounded carriage bodies have been located; several have been purchased, and some of these their new owners intend to rebuild to complete carriages.

The LBSCR was not at the forefront of carriage development at the Grouping in 1923. The railway had been building bogie coaches since the turn of the century, but at the Grouping had no ordinary corridor coaches and was still building coaches with the arc-profile roof; most large companies had long since adopted more 'modern' semi-elliptical profiles. The Brighton's only use of any sort of elliptical roof was in the 'balloon' coaches built for a period from about 1905; but these gave operational problems of loading gauge and the railway retreated to its familiar arc profiles for the rest of its independent existence. Though the LBSCR's loading gauge was generous, as its locomotives and Pullman coaches made clear, its ordinary service carriages were built to skimpy dimensions, and right to the end the bodies were rarely more than 8ft wide.

The LBSCR was a railway on which class distinctions were very evident in its train formations. The luxury and opulence of the all-Pullman 'Southern Belle' contrasted with the frugal appearance of its ordinary coaches, and often these two markedly contrasted types of carriage would appear in the same train, giving it a very 'mixed' appearance, with the ordinary carriages appearing distinctly undernourished.

The jobs of Locomotive Superintendent and Carriage and Wagon Superintendent were combined on the LBSCR until D.E. Marsh's retirement in 1911, when they were separated; A.H. Panter, carriage and wagon works manager since 1898 was then appointed Carriage and Wagon Superintendent, and retained this position until the Grouping. The five surviving carriages were all built in the 20th century, so they only represent the railway's final years – the oldest surviving LBSCR carriage is about ten years younger than the youngest surviving LBSCR locomotive. But the five survivors do cover a reasonable range of types, and probably give almost as good a cross section of 20th century LBSCR carriage practice as a mere five vehicles can. They range from a milk van to a directors saloon, and are carried variously on six, eight and twelve wheels. The absence of a 'balloon' coach is perhaps the most serious omission from the ranks.

The LBSCR numbered each main type of coach – firsts, seconds, thirds, composites – in a separate number series, and maintained this arrangement until the Grouping. The Southern then adopted a single number series for all its passenger carrying coaches with 'class' blocks of numbers, and another single series for non-passenger carrying vehicles; the ex-LBSCR coaches were in due course numbered into these series.

Luggage/Milk Van No. 270

The oldest preserved LBSCR carriage is a 6-wheel non-passenger carrying vehicle. This is a van of a pattern designed by R.J. Billinton for carrying luggage or for conveying a variety of perishable traffic including milk and fruit. It was equipped to run attached to passenger trains, and was built to the same profile as the railway's passenger coaching stock of the period. This pattern of van was built extensively by the LBSCR between 1896 and 1908. No. 270 was completed at Brighton Works in June 1908, so it is the only one of these preserved coaches to predate the railway's removal of its carriage and wagon works to Lancing. It was classified at first under LBSCR diagram 232, and later under diagram 229.

This type of van was the most numerous pattern of LBSCR luggage van at the Grouping, accounting for about two thirds of such vehicles taken over by the Southern from the LBSCR; they were classified as SR diagram 975. The 69 of these vehicles inherited by the Southern had been numbered within the ranges 201-300 and 501-518 in the LBSCR's list of passenger brake and luggage vans; the Southern renumbered them within the range 2082-2180 in their list of non-passenger carrying vehicles. Van No. 270 was renumbered as SR van No. 2178 in January 1927, and received vacuum brake at the same time. It was transferred to departmental use in 1939, and was renumbered 1525S and used at Lancing Works as a yard wagon for many years.

On a visit to Lancing Works in September 1963, a group of Bluebell RPS members inspected No. 1525S and another fairly similar vehicle, and they decided No. 1525S was in the better condition in view of the better state of its body work, with all original panelling and louvres intact. In the New Year a fund was established to raise the £150 purchase price quoted by BR, which was to include the cost of putting the vehicle into a condition to run. The purchase was completed in April 1964, and the van arrived on the Bluebell Railway on 13th May 1964, propelled over the line from Haywards Heath by the 'Terrier' No. 32636, also on its delivery run. This was the last train to run over the full Haywards Heath–Horsted Keynes section.

After its arrival at the Bluebell line, the van was given a handsome external restoration to its original LBSCR state as van No. 270. This was completed in 1966; since then the vehicle has been in use by the railway's Signals and Telecommunications department. However, as the restoration was external rather than structural the livery has deteriorated and the vehicle now awaits a complete overhaul.

Height 11'9"

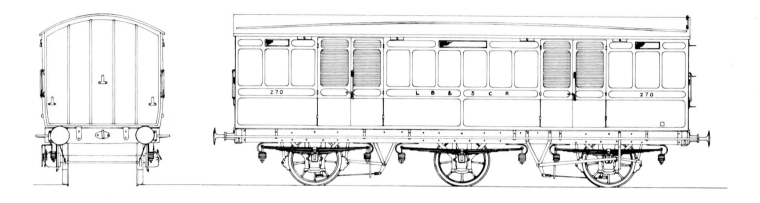

Above: The 6-wheel Milk Van preserved at the Bluebell Railway is of a pattern used for meat, milk, parcels, etc. *Gerry Bixley*

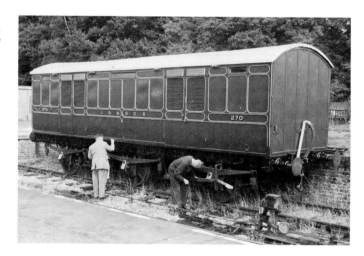

The preserved milk van has been restored to LBSCR brown livery as No. 270. Here it is receiving attention to details at Horsted Keynes. *Bluebell RPS Archives*

Length	. . . . 30ft. 0in	Completion date	. . . . June 1908
Width	. . . . 8ft. 0in.	Cost	. . . .£155-4-3
LBSCR Diagram No.	. . . . 232, later 229	Numbers:-	LBSCR – 270 (6/08)
SR Diagram No.	 975		SR – 2178 (1/27), 1525S (1939)
Weight	. . . . 11 tons		
Number of seats	. . . . None		

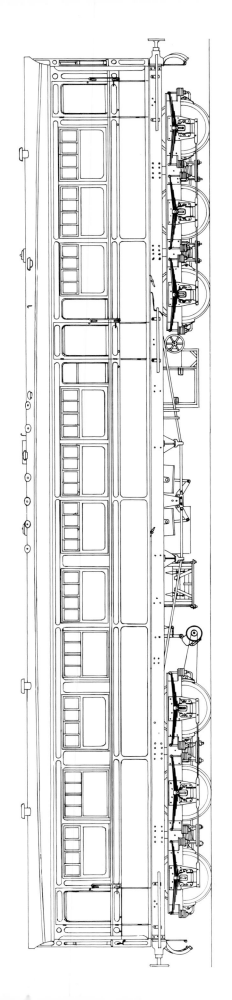

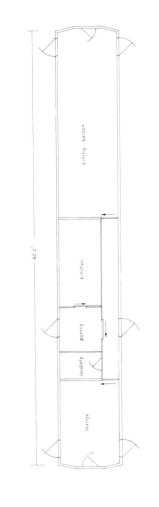

lounge | lavatory | pantry | kitchen | dining saloon

60' 0"

12' 2½"

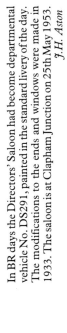

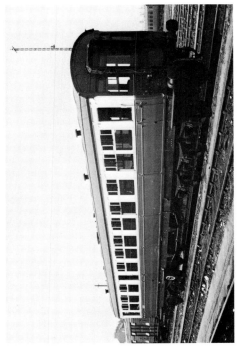

Above: The LBSCR Directors Saloon in all its splendour. This was a very long vehicle by the standards of normal LBSCR carriage stock.
Gerry Bixley

In BR days the Directors' Saloon had become departmental vehicle No. DS291, painted in the standard livery of the day. The modifications to the ends and windows were made in 1933. The saloon is at Clapham Junction on 25th May 1953.
J.H. Aston

First Class (Directors) Saloon No. 60

This is a very special carriage. It was completed in June 1914 at Lancing Works, and was intended for use by the directors and principal officers of the LBSCR. It was mounted on six-wheel bogies and was classified as diagram 67; the body was 8ft 6in wide, a little more generous than on the company's run-of-the-mill carriages, as was its length of 61ft (over bow ends).

Although completed structurally in 1914, the saloon was in store during the First World War and was fitted out internally in 1918. It had two main compartments (saloons), one large and one small, connected by a side corridor which gave access to lavatory, kitchen and pantry. The large saloon was furnished with two long tables and small chairs, allowing its use as board room or as dining room. The small saloon was more informally furnished with twelve lounge chairs, though seating capacity, in a vehicle without fixed seats, can vary a bit (officially it was quoted variously as 22 or 26 first class seats). The internal finish was of mahogany and satin wood, with Adam style ceiling decorations; clearly all was as it should be for Very Important People.

When the directors saloon passed into Southern Railway ownership in 1923, the new railway did not allocate this vehicle a number in ordinary running stock, as it was not a revenue earning vehicle. Instead it was classed as departmental stock, and given the number 291S; it was classified as diagram 1851. It was rebuilt in 1933, when the original windowed bow ends were altered with added corridor connections and new windows with sliding ventilators were fitted. In Southern days the saloon was used by the railway's senior officers, and was occasionally attached to the Royal Train.

Under British Railways, the saloon was renumbered DS291 and was based at Stewarts Lane for many years. It ran in the standard BR red and cream livery for about ten years, but was repainted in unlined green in November 1962, and was withdrawn in May 1965.

Before the saloon's withdrawal, the British Railways Board had considered preserving it, but later decided they were not able to do so. Instead they gave the Bluebell Railway first option to purchase this unique vehicle, and the railway were able to complete the purchase shortly afterwards; the saloon was moved to Haywards Heath late in June 1965 and to the Bluebell Railway on 4th August following.

As the saloon had been maintained in excellent condition, always being stored under cover, it was possible for it to enter service for its new owners immediately. It was then repainted in LBSCR umber livery and overhauled, including the removal of the corridor connections. It was painted olive drab for filming use in the late 1970s, and has since then been in store under cover. The necessary parts are being gathered together, with a view to restoring the carriage to its original condition.

Length	. . . . 61ft. 0in	Completion date	. . . . June 1914
Width	. . . . 8ft. 6in.	Cost	. . . . £2165-6-4
LBSCR Diagram No.	67	Numbers:-	LBSCR – 60 (6/14)
SR Diagram No.	1851		SR – 291S
Weight	. . . . 38 tons 8 cwt		BR – DS291
Number of seats	. . . . 22 or 26 first class		

One of the more splendid of preserved carriages is the LBSCR Directors' Saloon. It is shown here in its original condition in an official photograph.

R.C. Riley collection

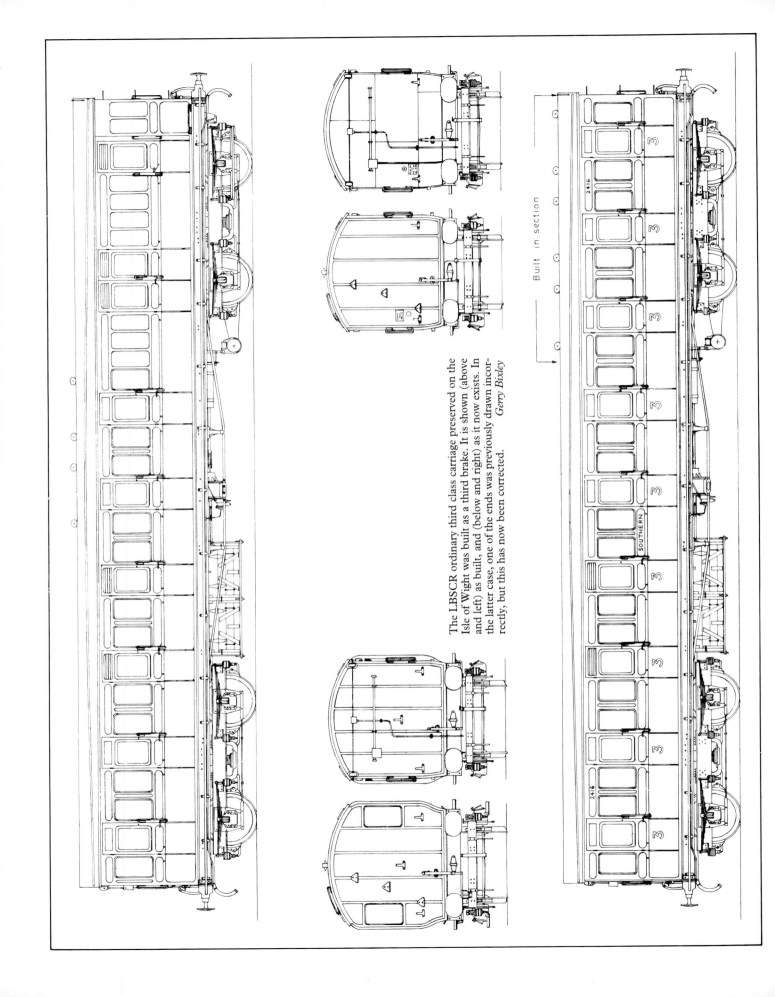

The LBSCR ordinary third class carriage preserved on the Isle of Wight was built as a third brake. It is shown (above and left) as built, and (below and right) as it now exists. In the latter case, one of the ends was previously drawn incorrectly, but this has now been corrected.

Gerry Bixley

Built in section

2416

SOUTHERN

Ordinary Passenger Carriages

When railway carriage preservation began on a significant scale, in the early 1960s, very few ordinary LBSCR passenger carriages remained in service on the mainland, and none was obtained for preservation. But many such coaches had been transferred to the Isle of Wight over the years, and some of these remained in service up to the end of steam on the Island at the end of 1966.

The Wight Locomotive Society bought three LBSCR coaches for £80 each in January 1967, when these coaches were lying out of use at Newport. When the Society established its operations at Havenstreet, the three LBSCR coaches formed the first of the four trains, worked by 'O2' class No. 24 *Calbourne* from Newport to Havenstreet, that constituted the Society's move to its new quarters on 24th January 1971. These three coaches then formed the first revenue earning train on the Isle of Wight Steam Railway on 12th April 1971, and they have been in regular use ever since.

The Isle of Wight Steam Railway only possesses a small number of vehicles, and so is very dependent on those few. The demands on these three LBSCR coaches have been heavy, and their record of availability for service has been exemplary. The three coaches were certainly not built as a set, though they are now often considered as one. They just happen to be three compatible coaches that go well together, and they will now be described individually.

Third Brake No. 641 (now ordinary third)

This carriage was completed at Lancing in June 1916, and was classified as LBSCR diagram 201; it was one of eighteen carriages to this pattern, which were numbered 636-650 and 851-853 in the railway's list of thirds and third brakes. These coaches each had 60 third class seats in six compartments, and a guards/brake and luggage compartment.

The eighteen coaches were renumbered 4014-4031 by the Southern Railway, and were assigned to diagram 203. No. 641 took up its allotted number 4019 in June 1927 and at the same time was fitted with vacuum brakes. It ran as part of SR set No. 861.

No. 4019 was transferred to the Isle of Wight in May 1936, and was radically rebuilt, the guards and luggage compartment being replaced by three third class passenger compartments, giving a new capacity of 90 third class seats in nine compartments. It was re-classified under diagram 90 at this point, and renumbered 2416. It remained at work on the Isle of Wight until it was withdrawn in January 1967 and purchased by the Wight Locomotive Society.

This carriage was the first to enter the new Havenstreet works on the Isle of Wight Steam Railway, for assorted repairs in the first half of 1981. Apart from this, No. 2416 has been in virtually continuous service since 1971, with only the winter months for maintenance.

Length	. . . .	54ft. 0in
Width	. . . .	8ft. 0in.
LBSCR Diagram No.	. . . .	201
SR Diagram No.	. . . .	203, later 90
Weight	. . . .	24 tons
Number of seats	. . . .	60 third class,
	. . . .	later 90 third class

Completion date	. . . .	June 1916
Cost	. . . .	£855-0-0
Numbers:-	LBSCR – 641 (6/16)	
	SR – 4019 (6/27), 2416 (5/36)	

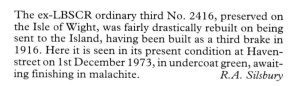
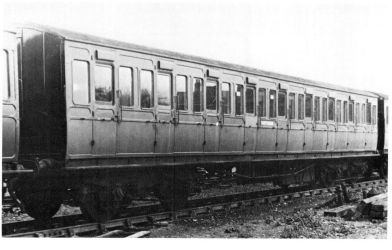

The ex-LBSCR ordinary third No. 2416, preserved on the Isle of Wight, was fairly drastically rebuilt on being sent to the Island, having been built as a third brake in 1916. Here it is seen in its present condition at Havenstreet on 1st December 1973, in undercoat green, awaiting finishing in malachite.   *R.A. Silsbury*

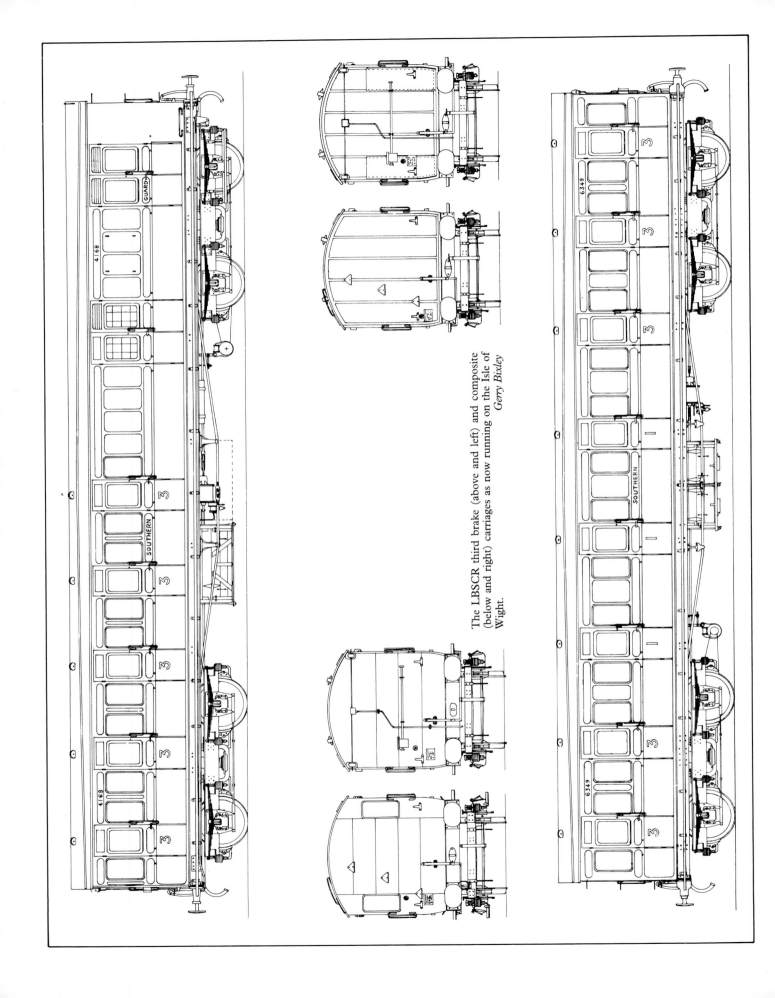

The LBSCR third brake (above and left) and composite (below and right) carriages as now running on the Isle of Wight.

Gerry Bixley

Third Brake No. 93

This was one of ten carriages classified as LBSCR diagram 141, and numbered between 82 and 112 in the railway's list of thirds and third brakes. These coaches had 50 third class seats in five compartments, plus guards/brake compartment. No. 93 was completed at Lancing in June 1922, and made use of a previously used underframe dating from 1905. The ten coaches to this pattern were allocated Southern Railway diagram No. 198, and became SR Nos. 3866-3872 and 3874-3876; No. 93 became SR No. 3870 in May 1924 and received vacuum brake in October 1925. No. 3870 was part of SR 3-car set No. 825.

No. 3870 was transferred to the Isle of Wight in April 1938, and though no structural changes were made it was reclassified as diagram 230; at the same time it was renumbered into the Isle of Wight series as No. 4168. It was in service up to the end of steam on the Isle of Wight, and was included in the last steam hauled passenger train from Shanklin to Ryde. It was withdrawn in January 1967 and purchased by the Wight Locomotive Society.

Apart from a few trains in 1971 and two Sundays in 1980, this carriage has been used in every IWSR passenger train since operations started; this included its use on the late Earl Mountbatten of Burma's special train on 22nd January 1976. This continuous use has been because this is the only vehicle on the line which has both guard's accommodation and passenger seats fit for use. However, one of the railway's ex-SECR third brakes has now completed an overhaul, and should be able to ease the load on carriage No. 4168.

Length	. . . . 54ft. 0in	Completion date	. . . . .June 1922
Width	. . . . 8ft. 0in.	Cost	. . . .£1782-5-9
LBSCR Diagram No.	. . . .?	Numbers:-	LBSCR – 93 (6/22)
SR Diagram No.	. . . . .198, later 230		SR – 3870 (5/24), 4168 (4/38)
Weight	. . . . .24 tons		
Number of seats	. . . . 50 third class		

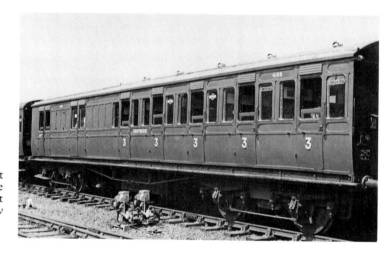

The ex-LBSCR third brake No. 4168 has been in almost continuous service on the Isle of Wight Steam Railway since the railway opened. Here the vehicle is at rest at Havenstreet on 19th July 1984.   *R.A. Silsbury*

First/Third Composite No. 7

This was the LBSCR's allocated number for this carriage, which it did not carry as it was not completed at Lancing until February 1924. It originally had four first class compartments, giving 24 seats, flanked by four third class compartments giving 40 seats. It was one of ten carriages built to this pattern. The Southern Railway assigned Nos. 6162-6171 to these ten coaches, and classified them as diagram 337. The preserved coach ran as SR No. 6164 from the start, and was fitted with vacuum brake in June 1926.

Nine of the ten diagram 337 coaches went to the Isle of Wight, and No. 6164 was one of the batch which were sent there in March 1937. On arrival, one of the four first class compartments was downgraded to third, so the carriage now had 50 third class seats, and in this new configuration it was classified as diagram 373; it was also renumbered 6349 in the Isle of Wight series. It was in service almost to the end of steam on the island, being withdrawn in November 1966 and was subsequently bought by the Wight Locomotive Society.

No. 6349 was out of service for an extensive overhaul between Spring 1982 and July 1983, but otherwise has been in regular use on the Isle of Wight Steam Railway.

Length	.... 54ft. 0in	later	...............18 first class,
Width	.... 8ft. 0in.		.... 50 third class.
LBSCR Diagram No.	..........................?	Completion date	.... February 1924
SR Diagram No.	....................337, later 373	Cost	
Weight	.... 26 tons	Numbers:-	LBSCR – 7 (never carried)
Number of seats	.... 24 first class,		SR – 6164 (2/24), 6349 (3/37)
	.... 40 third class.		

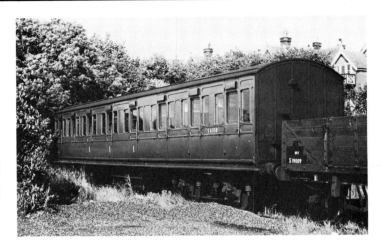

The ex-LBSCR composite carriage on the Isle of Wight Steam Railway is one of a batch which were altered on being sent to the Island, only to the extent of one first class compartment being downgraded to third. The preserved coach is No. 6349; this is No. 6350 of the same batch, at Sandown on 28th June 1958.   *J.H. Aston*

Grounded Bodies

From about 1920, and maybe even earlier, Lancing Works sold off a large number of bodies of withdrawn carriages and vans, which were then put to a wide variety of uses, such as conversion to chalets and bungalows. Many of these found their new homes at locations along the south coast, and after many years most of them have deteriorated badly. But a few have been located which are still in good enough condition to be worth buying; the body is then bought, restored and placed on 'new' underframes, thereby adding to the range of restored LBSCR carriages.

First class No. 667 was built by Brown Marshalls in 1880 and later became brake second No. 262 and then brake third No. 1648. It was withdrawn in 1920 and its body was sold for use in a bungalow at Wittering. It was still in remarkably good condition when rescued by the Bluebell Railway and taken to Horsted Keynes in April 1983. It is stored awaiting restoration with a suitable underframe.

First class No. 142 was built in 1902 and entered service the following year. It became Southern Railway No. 7598, and was withdrawn in 1931. Its body was then moved to West Chiltington, near Storrington, and, as a roof was put over it, it remained in good condition. It was used at first as a dwelling, but latterly as an aviary. It was donated to the Bluebell Railway and moved to Horsted Keynes on 6th September 1989; given a suitable underframe, it is planned to restore it to running order.

Third class No. 20 was built by the LBSCR in 1896, becoming No. 1520 in 1911 and SR (mainland) No. 1840. It went to the Isle of Wight in 1925 as No. 2343

and it was withdrawn in 1931 and its body sold for use as a chalet at Gurnard. It was later donated to the Wight Locomotive Society and arrived at Havenstreet in July 1984. It is stored in the open pending restoration on a suitable underframe.

A number of LBSCR grounded bodies survive on Hayling Island; the distinctly 'holiday' nature of this island led to a sizeable requirement for bungalows, chalets, etc. for holiday accommodation, and grounded carriage bodies were often used in this role.

First class No. 660 is a Stroudley 6-wheel vehicle built by Brown Marshalls in 1880. It was modified to become brake second No. 261 in 1908, and it was reclassified again in 1911 to become brake third No. 1646. It is currently being restored by the Hayling Island Railway Society. They are also planning to re-store former 6-wheel first class No. 521, which was modified to become tri-composite No. 98 in 1908 and was reclassified as composite in 1911. These two coach bodies were sold by the LBSCR and moved to Hayling Island in 1921. They were used together as a bungalow, and later as a chalet, before being donated to the Hayling Island Railway Society in 1986.

Other ex-LBSCR coach bodies on Hayling Island include 4-wheel composite No. 194 of 1879, and another Stroudley 4-wheel body, latterly third No. 1636; the latter, however, is probably only useable as a source of spare parts. Another coach body planned for restoration by the Hayling Island Railway Society is Stroudley full brake No. 174, sold in 1920 and resident near Pulborough for many years.

Preserved LBSCR Wagons

All drawings to 4mm scale

The preserved LBSCR wagons all date from the later years of the railway; none are earlier than about 1900, and most are from the Marsh and A.H. Panter superintendencies. But LBSCR wagons did not alter very much over the years so, though no Stroudley vehicles remain, the survivors are very much in the Stroudley manner. Open wagons represented by far the largest part of the LBSCR's goods stock at the Grouping; this is reflected in the vehicles preserved, which at the same time do present a reasonable variety.

As with LBSCR preserved carriages, so too with wagons – more than half are on the Isle of Wight. A large number of LBSCR wagons were sent to the Island by the Southern Railway, and some of them continued in regular use there up to the end of steam in 1966, and in

some cases after that. This meant that the Wight Locomotive Society and other groups were able to obtain some very attractive items; the list of mainland vehicles is a bit thin.

As preserved wagons are unlikely to contribute much to the revenue of a steam railway, they tend to take a low priority in the allocation of resources for preservation. In the case of several LBSCR wagons this has meant that they have not been able to receive the attention their historical value merits, and as a result the condition of some of them has deteriorated. This raises a basic question about wagon preservation - it has to be an altruistic, educational exercise, so how is the necessary effort and expense to be justified?

Closed Vans

The LBSCR never possessed a large number of covered vans, only owning about 600 at the Grouping. The design remained essentially the same for very many years; vans built at the end of the railway's independent existence were recognisably the same pattern as Stroudley had built in the 1870s, though some minor changes had been made.

No. 8195 is an 8 ton capacity van built by the LBSCR around 1900. It was renumbered 46543 by the Southern Railway in May 1928, and classified under diagram 1433. At some later date it was sold to Chatham Dockyard where it was renumbered 590. It stayed there until found by a group of supporters of the Bluebell Railway, who bought it and took it to their line

in June 1981; it awaits restoration.

Van No. 3713 was built by the LBSCR in 1920, and being a 10 ton capacity van was classified by the Southern under diagram 1436. It was renumbered 46773 in November 1929. It was then transferred to departmental use as an S&T store van, numbered 1188S, in October 1937, but returned to running stock as 46773 once more in January 1939. During the war it returned to departmental service again as No. 1704S and after the war was based for many years at Crabtree Sidings, Belvedere, where side windows were cut in it. It was purchased by the Tenterden Rolling Stock Group and moved to Tenterden on 11th November 1978. An extensive programme of restoration is planned.

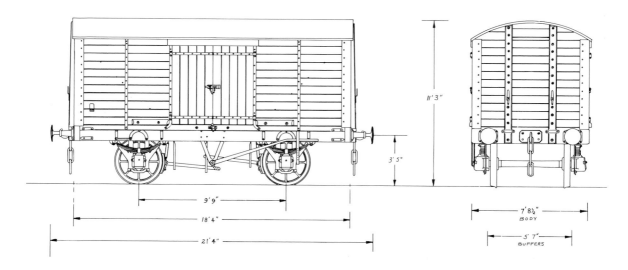

This is the typical pattern of an LBSCR closed goods van. Both the preserved examples are very similar to this.

Gerry Bixley

Covered vans

SR diagram .... 1433 etc (see text)	Rated capacity .... (see text)
Length over headstocks .... 18ft. 4in.	Length over buffers .... 21ft. 4in.
Wheelbase .... 9ft. 9in.	Width .... 7ft. 10in.

Typical of the LBSCR pattern of covered van is 8 ton van No. 590, formerly at Chatham Dockyard. This was its appearance at the time of sale to the Bluebell Railway in 1981. *M.J. Allen*

The 10 ton capacity covered van formerly at Crabtree Sidings, Belvedere, went to the Kent & East Sussex Railway in 1978, and is seen at Tenterden on 31st August 1980. Side windows have been cut, and the body needs some repairs. *Paul Ramsden*

Covered Van (former cattle wagon)

Its origins make this vehicle look a lot different from the standard pattern of LBSCR covered van. It was built in 1922 as cattle wagon No. 7116, and was classified by the Southern Railway under diagram 1528 and allocated No. 53291. But it probably never carried this number, as it was transferred to the Isle of Wight in August 1927 and renumbered 53374. It was one of six LBSCR cattle wagons sent to the Island in 1927-29, but three of these, including this wagon, were deemed surplus to livestock carrying requirements and converted to ordinary covered vans in August 1935. So cattle wagon No. 53374 became covered van No. 46924, reclassified under diagram 1457. In 1948 it was transferred to departmental use as S&T stores van No. 1066S.

Following the end of steam on the Island in 1967, this wagon was included in the National Collection of preserved railway vehicles, and was moved to store at Fratton in May 1967, and then to Preston Park in November of that year. In 1977 the Wight Locomotive Society negotiated the loan of this interesting vehicle, and it returned to the Isle of Wight on 21st March 1978. It has since been restored to SR brown livery, and remains the only National Collection wagon on loan to an outside society; it has been fitted with air brakes and is sometimes used on passenger trains.

Covered (ex-cattle) wagon

SR diagram	1457	Rated capacity	10 tons
Length over headstocks	18ft. 4in.	Length over buffers	21ft. 4in.
Wheelbase	11ft. 2in.	Width	8ft. 1¾in.

A quite untypical LBSCR covered van is the preserved former cattle wagon, which served its later years on the Isle of Wight, and which now belongs to the National Collection. It is seen carrying little trace of any paint, and with the number 46924, which it carried after conversion in 1935, painted on rather roughly.   *T.P. Cooper*

The ex-cattle wagon was restored in SR brown livery, and is seen at Havenstreet on 19th July 1984.   *R.A. Silsbury*

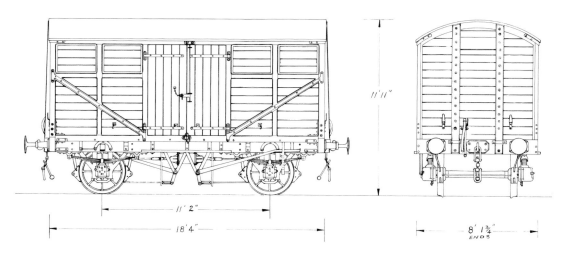

The former cattle wagon, now converted to a closed van, is very different from the typical LBSCR closed van.   *Gerry Bixley*

Single Bolster Wagons

Wagons of this type were mostly used in combinations of two or more to carry long loads; the main commercial need was for carrying tree trunks, baulks of timber and similar items, and they were also used to carry rails. The LBSCR also built some double bolster wagons, but unlike many other railways did not build bogie bolster wagons.

These surviving bolster wagons are among the oldest of the preserved LBSCR wagons. They were classified as diagram 1616 by the Southern, and these three (and two others still on BR's books on the Island) are the survivors of fifteen such wagons sent to the Isle of Wight in 1928 and 1930. Following the end of steam on the Island these three wagons were among a number reserved for Vectrail. They were moved from Ryde to Newport in July 1969, and to Havenstreet on 24th January 1971; they were donated to the Wight Locomotive Society in 1971.

LBSCR wagon No. 4659 was built at Lancing in 1909 and was allocated SR No. 58358; it was sent to the Isle of Wight in May 1928 and renumbered 59038. It has not been restored, and is now in rather poor condition.

Wagon No. 4552 was built in 1910 and became SR No. 58299, going to the Island in February 1930 and being renumbered 59049. It has not been restored.

No. 4631 was also built in 1910 and its SR (mainland) number was 58341. It went to the Island in March 1930 and was renumbered 59050. It has been restored to SR brown livery, the job being completed in January 1984.

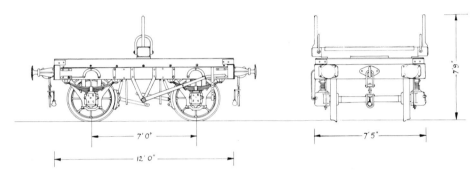

Three of this pattern of LBSCR single bolster wagon are preserved on the Isle of Wight, and two more remain in BR departmental service.
Gerry Bixley

Bolster wagons

SR diagram 1616	Rated capacity . . . . .6 tons
Length over headstocks . . . . 12ft. 0in.	Length over buffers . . . . .15ft. 0in.
Wheelbase . . . . 7ft. 0in.	Width . . . . .7ft. 5in.

Only one of the Isle of Wight Steam Railway's three single bolster wagons has been restored. This is No. 59050, seen at Wootton on 15th September 1987.
P. Cooper

Road Vehicle Truck

Wagons like this were built for the carriage of road vehicles, when this was a better way of conveying them over long distances than using the poorly made roads of the time. The survivor was built at Lancing in 1923 as LBSCR No. 7129. The Southern classified it under diagram 1661, and allocated the number 60536, but this was not carried as the vehicle was sent to the Isle of Wight in August 1929 and renumbered 60579.

It remained in service up to the end of steam on the Island, and was purchased for the Wight Locomotive Society for £50 in August 1968. It was moved by road to Newport on 26th July 1969 and by rail to Havenstreet in the 'great move' of 24th January 1971. It has not been restored.

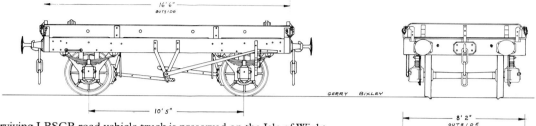

The only surviving LBSCR road vehicle truck is preserved on the Isle of Wight.   *Gerry Bixley*

Road vehicle truck	
SR diagram 1661	Rated capacity .... 10 tons
Length over headstocks .... 16ft. 6in.	Length over buffers .... 19ft. 6in.
Wheelbase .... 10ft. 5in.	Width .... 8ft. 2in.

The only surviving LBSCR road vehicle truck is No. 60579, seen in departmental use in 1962, in the old FYNR yard at Newport.   *R.A. Silsbury*

Open Wagons

This was the simplest and most basic form of railway vehicle and, as with so many railways, by far the preponderant type of wagon. On the LBSCR this was even more true than on most railways, as they accounted for about three quarters of the railway's wagon stock. Partly this was because many LBSCR open wagons were built with round ends and a sheet rail which, with a tarpaulin draped over the rail, could give the effect of a simple form of covered van. In Southern days (and even in the last days of the LBSCR) most of these curved ends, and the sheet rails, were removed to leave a normal square ended open wagon – in SR terms this typically meant reclassification from diagram 1369 to diagram 1364. Over 450 LBSCR open wagons were transferred to the Isle of Wight between 1924 and 1931, and a high proportion of the survivors were among these.

Some of the preserved LBSCR open wagons are of the normal form, with the door in the middle section of the wagon side. Open wagon No. 3537 was built in 1912 and was renumbered 22696 by the Southern. On transfer to the Isle of Wight it was renumbered 27884 and it remained in service until the end of steam on the Island.

It was then assigned to the National Collection, and returned to the mainland to store at Fratton in May 1967. It moved on to Preston Park in November 1967 and was then moved to the National Railway Museum at York. It has not been restored and is not currently on public view.

Wagon No. 3346 was built in 1914 and became Southern Railway No. 22568. It was later sold to the Longmoor Military Railway where it became No. AD46269. When the Longmoor Military Railway closed in 1969 the wagon was sold and went to Liss. When it became available for resale it was bought by the Bluebell Railway and arrived on their line in February 1974. It arrived in the typical square-ended form, and in fairly tatty condition. It was then handsomely restored to round ended condition, with sheet rail, and LBSCR grey livery; it then accompanied the 'Terrier' *Fenchurch* to the Stockton and Darlington 150th anniversary celebrations at Shildon in August 1975.

The next two of these open wagons are on the Isle of Wight, where they have been for over 50 years. Both were withdrawn by BR at the end of steam on the Island, and were reserved for use by Vectrail but were later taken over by the Wight Locomotive Society. They were moved from Ryde to Newport in July 1969 and to Havenstreet in January 1971. The first of these two was LBSCR No. 8511, completed at Lancing in April 1924, which became SR (mainland) No. 26173 and then No. 28346 on transfer to the Isle of Wight in May 1927. It was then transferred to departmental stock as DS64396 in August 1959. The other wagon did not carry an LBSCR number, as it was completed in March 1925 and was SR No. 27696 from the start, becoming No. 27834 on transfer to the Island in June 1931. No. 27834 has been cosmetically restored, but No. DS64396 was cut up late in 1989, with the intention of using the parts to refurbish other Island open wagons.

The histories of the next two open wagons are not fully known, both having been bought from military use; in this case it is often difficult to trace the origins of a wagon.

No. AD46054 was purchased from MoD Bicester and moved to Quainton Road in July 1971. It has not been restored.

An unnumbered wagon at Telford Horsehay, bought from the MoD in 1984, was previously thought to be of LSWR origin, but is now known to be an LBSCR wagon.

Open wagons

SR diagram	1369 etc	Rated capacity	10 tons etc.
Length over headstocks	15ft. 5in.	Length over buffers	18ft. 5in.
Wheelbase	9ft. 3in.	Width	7ft. 9n.

The only LBSCR open wagon which has received the full restoration treatment is No. 3346 at the Bluebell Railway. The rounded ends have been restored, decayed parts replaced, and the repainted vehicle attended the 1975 Shildon cavalcade. It is seen in the exhibition hall at Shildon Works at that time.   *R. John*

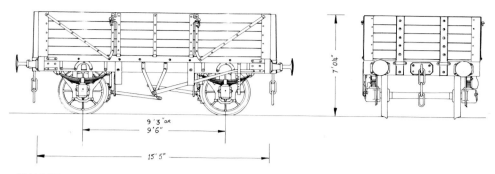

The typical pattern of LBSCR open wagon as most of them are now running.

Gerry Bixley

In addition to these six wagons there are four preserved dropside open wagons, converted from ordinary open wagons on the Isle of Wight around the time of the end of steam in 1966. A small fleet of dropside wagons was retained at this point, the majority of them being of LBSCR origin. The parts used for these conversions were mostly of SECR derivation, being originally contractors' vehicles, so the resulting dropside wagons are of distinctly mixed pedigree. As these wagons became surplus to BR needs they were made available for sale and some of them were purchased for preservation. The first two were sold by BR in 1973 and were purchased by the Wight Locomotive Society and moved to Havenstreet. Neither of these ever had an LBSCR number; the first was completed in July 1924 as SR No. 27520, and became No. 27766 on transfer to the Island in June 1930. The second was completed in August 1925 as SR No. 18803, and became No. 28345 on transfer to the Isle of Wight in May 1927. Both these wagons remain in sound condition.

Right: The surviving LBSCR ordinary open wagon on the Isle of Wight Steam Railway has been cosmetically restored. This is No. 27834, seen in 'as transferred' livery, Lancing style, at Havenstreet on 22nd August 1974.
R.A. Silsbury

Below: The LBSCR open wagon No. AD46054 at Quainton Road has not been restored, and remains in a nondescript military livery. It is seen in use for storage of rough pieces of timber, with 'LOCO COAL' rather incongruously written on the other side. 16th August 1987.
P. Cooper

Below right: The unnumbered wagon at Telford was previously credited as being ex-LSWR, but is now known to be ex-LBSCR.
J.R. Fairman

The other two dropside wagons were sold rather later; they were of relatively late build, so they did not have LBSCR numbers, and it is believed they were converted to dropside rather later than the previous two. Wagon No. 18928 was built in August 1925 and was renumbered 27730 on transfer to the Isle of Wight in April 1930. After withdrawal it was sold to the Bluebell Railway, and it arrived on their line in July 1980.

Wagon No. 18930 was also completed in 1925, and became No. 27744 on transfer to the Isle of Wight in May 1930. After withdrawal it was sold to the Southern Steam Trust and went to the Swanage Railway in 1980, but it was later resold to the Wight Locomotive Society and returned to the Isle of Wight, arriving at Havenstreet in November 1983. It is now (early 1990) being rebuilt back to its original form, using parts from the dismantled No. DS64396.

Above: Four of the ex-LBSCR open wagons converted to drop-side form on the Isle of Wight survive in preservation. The only one on the mainland is No. 27730 (above left) at Horsted Keynes on 30th August 1987. *(P. Cooper)* The other three are on the Isle of Wight – No. 27744 (above right) *(P.J. Relf)* and Nos. 28345 and 27766 both at Wootton on 15th September 1987. *(P. Cooper)*

Right: The only LBSCR wagons to survive in any sort of BR service are two single bolsters, Nos. DS59043 and DS59045. The two are seen parked in a siding at Sandown, Isle of Wight, on 17th September 1987.   *P. Cooper*

Still Serving...

The military bought a large number of pregouping wagons over the years, and these included some of LBSCR origin. Exactly what was bought, and what remains, is not known, as there are few records available and access to the relevant depots is restricted. A 1970s list includes only a small number of LBSCR wagons:-
Flat wagons No. 40111 (ex open wagon 46182) and No. 40115 (ex closed van 47448), both at Long Marston
Open wagon No. 46269, which went to the Bluebell Railway
Closed vans No. 47456, thought to be at Bicester, and No. 47655, formerly at Kineton.

This gives only Army wagons; certain Navy establishments may also have a few.

Two LBSCR wagons remained in BR service in 1989, though it is believed neither has turned a wheel for several years. These are bolster wagons Nos. ADS59043 and ADS 59045, which are parked at Sandown, Isle of Wight; both went to the Island in June 1928, when they took their present numbers, but without the departmental 'ADS' prefixes. No. 59043 was built in 1907 as LBSCR No. 4545, and became SR mainland No. 58296; No. 59045 was built in 1911 as LBSCR No. 7317 and became mainland No. 58443. They are the same pattern as the three bolster wagons preserved by the Wight Locomotive Society.

Appendix I

Allocations since 1933

From 1933 onward, reasonably complete allocation histories can be given for the preserved locomotives. As with so many such things, we mainly have to thank the RCTS's Railway Observer for making this possible. The initial allocation is at January 1933.

No.	Allocation
40	Newport, Fratton (6/47), Rolvenden (7/48), Newhaven (3/51), Eastleigh (stored, 10/51), Fratton (stored, 5/52), St. Leonards (8/52), Newhaven (9/52), Fratton (5/54), Brighton (9/55), Fratton (5/56), Eastleigh (11/59), Brighton (5/63), (Wdn 9/63)
46	Newport, Fratton (6/49), Newhaven (8/51), Fratton (8/53), Newhaven (5/54), Brighton (8/55), Fratton (5/56), Eastleigh (11/59) (Wdn 11/63)
50	Ryde, Lancing Carriage Works (4/37), Fratton (11/53), Eastleigh (11/59), (Wdn 11/63)
54	Lancing Carriage Works, (Wdn 2/63)
55	Fratton, Rolvenden (4/53), St. Leonards (1/54), Brighton (10/55), Eastleigh (2/60), (Wdn 5/60)
62	Fratton, St. Leonards (stored, 9/53), Newhaven (stored, 12/53), St. Leonards (stored, 9/54), Newhaven (7/55), Brighton (9/55), Eastleigh (5/63), (Wdn 11/63)
70	K&ESR, Rolvenden (1/48), St. Leonards (7/54), Brighton (1/58), Eastleigh (5/63), (Wdn 11/63)
72	Newhaven, Brighton (9/55), St. Leonards (10/55), Ashford (6/58), Fratton (9/59), Eastleigh (11/59), Brighton (2/60), Eastleigh (6/63), (Wdn 11/63)
78	Newport, Fratton (6/37), K&ESR (2/40), Rolvenden (1/48), St. Leonards (1/54), Fratton (6/58), Eastleigh (11/59), Brighton (5/63), (Wdn 10/63)
82	Brighton Works, (Wdn 8/46)
110	Cannock Colliery, (Wdn 5/63 approx.)
473	New Cross, Bricklayers Arms (about 1934), Brighton (5/35), Norwood Junction (during war),

Appendix II

Whereabouts since withdrawal

Since withdrawal the preserved locomotives have found themselves at a variety of locations, as follows:-

No.	Location
(326)40	Eastleigh (9/63), Butlins, Pwllheli (7/64), Ryde (1/73), Havenstreet (1/75)
(326)46	Eastleigh (11/63), Droxford (11/64), Hayling Island (5/66), Havenstreet (6/79)
(326)50	Eastleigh (11/63), K&ESR (9/64)
54/DS680	Eastleigh (2/63), St Constant, Canada (9/63)
(326)55	Eastleigh (5/60), Bluebell Railway (5/60)
(326)62	Fratton (11/63), Eastleigh (1/64), Butlins, Heads of Ayr (10/64), Bressingham (3/71)
(326)70	Eastleigh (11/63), K&ESR (4/64)
72/32636	Fratton (11/63), Eastleigh (1/64), Bluebell Railway (5/64)
(326)78	Eastleigh (10/63), Butlins, Minehead (7/64), W. Somerset Rly (3/75), Resco, Woolwich (4/83), K&ESR (1988)
82/380S	Brighton (8/46), Nine Elms (9/47), Farnham (7/48), Salisbury (?during 1950s), Tweedmouth (4/58), Eastleigh (8/59), Clapham (1/61), York (4/75)
110	Rawnsley (5/63), Hednesford (12/63), Chasewater (6/70), E. Somerset Rly (9/78)
214	Brighton (4/27), York (5/27), Reedsmouth (1941), York (1945 approx.)
(32)473	Nine Elms (10/62), Bluebell Railway (10/62)

Appendix III

Locations of preserved LBSCR rolling stock

Not all these items are on view or normally accessible by the public. Original LBSCR numbers are shown where they are known – other numbers are bracketted.

Location	Locomotives	Carriages	Wagons
National Railway Museum	'A' class No. 82 'B' class No. 214		Open wagon No. 3537
Bluebell Railway	'A' class No. 55 'A' class No. 72 'E4' class No. 473	First (saloon) No. 60 Luggage van No. 270	Open wagon No. 3346 Covered van No. 8195 Dropside open (No. 27730)
Isle of Wight Steam Railway	'A' class No. 40 'A' class No. 46	Third (No. 2416) Third brake No. 93 Composite No. 7	Covered van No. 7116 Road veh. truck No. 7129 Bolster wagon No. 4552 Bolster wagon No. 4631 Bolster wagon No. 4659 Open wagon (No. 27696) Dropside open (No. 27744) Dropsie open (No. 27766) Dropside open (No. 28345)
Kent and East Sussex	'A' class No. 50 'A' class No. 70 'A' class No. 78		Covered van No. 3713
Bressingham	'A' class No. 62		
E. Somerset	'E' class No. 110		
Quainton Rd			Open wagon (No. 46054)
Telford			Open wagon (No. ?)
and 'A' class No. 54 is in Canada.			

Acknowledgements

Preparing a book of this nature inevitably involves referring to a wide range of documents, and obtaining information from a large number of people. So the list of acknowledgements below may not be absolutely complete, but it certainly lists the people (and other sources) to whom I am most indebted. My apologies to anyone I have missed out.

Original documents at the Public Record Office, Kew, were referred to, and the Library staff of the National Railway Museum at York were, as always, very helpful in supplying data and photographs. The two periodicals I am most indebted to are the RCTS Railway Observer and Bluebell News, though others were referred to. The most valuable books have been 'Locomotives of the LBSCR' (D.L. Bradley – RCTS – 3 vols), 'Southern Wagons – Vol 2' (OPC) and 'The Brighton Gladstones' by Brian Reid (Profile Publications).

A number of preservation societies have also helped in the production of this book. The stock books of the Bluebell Railway, the Isle of Wight Steam Railway, and the Kent & East Sussex Railway were very valuable, and other information was supplied by members of the Bressingham Steam Museum Trust, Canadian Railway Historical Association, West Somerset Railway, Tenterden Railway Company, Chasewater Light Railway & Museum Co, East Somerset Railway and the Hayling Island Railway Society.

I must give particular thanks to Mr Gerry Bixley, whose drawings form a major part of the carriage and wagon sections of the book, and I am grateful for information on carriages and wagons from Messrs Mike King and Roger Silsbury. I must also thank Mr Klaus Marx for letting me dip at will into a full set of Bluebell News and to Mr Nick Felton for some valuable notes on Isle of Wight items. Finally, I must thank Mr R.C. Riley for reading the typescript and making a number of valuable suggestions.

A large part of the book is its photographic content. I would like to thank all those who supplied photographs and let me use them. Their contribution provides a historical record that speaks for itself; I hope the text provides an adequate accompaniment to this record.